Management Lessons
of a Failed Company

This book is part of the Peter Lang Political Science, Economics, and Law list.
Every volume is peer reviewed and meets the highest
quality standards for content and production.

PETER LANG
New York • Bern • Berlin
Brussels • Vienna • Oxford • Warsaw

Christopher M. Tingley

Management Lessons
of a Failed Company

PETER LANG
New York • Bern • Berlin
Brussels • Vienna • Oxford • Warsaw

Library of Congress Cataloging-in-Publication Data

Names: Tingley, Christopher M., author.
Title: Management lessons of a failed company / Christopher M. Tingley.
Description: New York: Peter Lang, 2021.
Identifiers: LCCN 2020052454 (print) | LCCN 2020052455 (ebook)
ISBN 978-1-4331-8484-0 (hardback) | ISBN 978-1-4331-8485-7 (ebook pdf)
ISBN 978-1-4331-8486-4 (epub) | ISBN 978-1-4331-8487-1 (mobi)
Subjects: LCSH: Tingley, Christopher M. | Steve & Barry's
(Department store) | Clothing trade—United States—Management—Case
studies. | Retail trade—United States—Management—Case studies. |
Business failures—United States—Case studies.
Classification: LCC HD9940.U4 T56 2021 (print) | LCC HD9940.U4 (ebook) |
DDC 381/.456870973—dc23
LC record available at https://lccn.loc.gov/2020052454
LC ebook record available at https://lccn.loc.gov/2020052455
DOI 10.3726/b18453

Bibliographic information published by **Die Deutsche Nationalbibliothek.**
Die Deutsche Nationalbibliothek lists this publication in the
"DeutscheNationalbibliografie"; detailed bibliographic data are available
on the Internet at http://dnb.d-nb.de/.

© 2021 Peter Lang Publishing, Inc., New York
80 Broad Street, 5th floor, New York, NY 10004
www.peterlang.com

The names of the store employees and managers have been changed to allow for anonymity. The narrative in this book is recalled to the best of the author's recollection. No disparagement of the owners, employees or partners was intentional.

Contents

Introduction

In July of 2006, I had just recently completed my MBA. I had graduated 2 years earlier with a bachelor's degree in communication arts, and I wanted to add a level of business acumen to my resume. I might have been young at this time, but I felt like I was well prepared and was ready to become part of the business world. I had been employed full time since my sophomore year in high school working in kitchens, video stores, and in radio. I cut my hair short, put away my black t-shirts sporting heavy metal band logos and packed my bags. I moved south where I wouldn't have to see snow ever again.

I had been told throughout my education that there were jobs available and all it took was a good degree, hard work and dedication to make a career for myself. My professors told me that an MBA was a direct ticket to employment. I was confident that, despite moving to a new city away from home, all I had to do was walk in and tell people I had an MBA and they would hire me. I had my elevator speech ready to go, armed with my sales pitch of a communications background and a master's degree in business. I knew that no one would ever say no to me.

In fact, I was convinced that companies would not only hire me, but they would pay me an incredible amount of money and give me every-thing I wanted. At the time, it felt like I had nothing but opportunities ahead of me and a bright future to look forward to. I remember think-ing I could smell the interior of the imported sports car I assumed my future salary would provide.

After making it to my new home, I looked in the classified ads and found an opening only a few miles from my apartment. I was quickly hired to work as a commissioned salesman at a small car dealership that sold a national brand name of cars. I wasn't hired because of any of my education, experience, or sales knowledge. The sales manager, a Marine Corps veteran who wore a large gold ring symbolizing his sales success, heard me speak in my interview. He asked "Is your voice always that loud? If so, you have a job here."

I took the job selling cars. I assumed I'd be great at it. While I was employed there I learned all about how to sell, and how to get a cus-tomer to sign on the dotted line. I must have watched that famous movie scene a dozen times saying to "always be closing." Some of what I learned might have been slightly outside my usual ethical threshold, but I knew I had to do what was necessary if I wanted to pay the rent.

I was never happy being a car salesman. I hated the looks people would give me when I told them what I did for a living. I hated the long days of waiting around for a customer to walk on the lot. The car manufacturer I worked for had been repositioning themselves as a higher quality car brand, which seemed good in theory, but rarely led to interested buyers. We had a lot of window shoppers who had very little interest in purchasing any of our inventory.

In early October 2006, an up-and-coming new retailer, Steve and Barry's University Sportswear, offered me a job as a store manager. I put in my two-week notice at the car dealership. I had always adhered to the tradition of giving proper notice when resigning from a job. The sales manager thanked me for my time but said "Look kid, in this busi-ness, there is no such thing as a two-week notice. Go ahead and leave, and don't talk to anyone on your way out." I went home and packed my bags and got ready for a 2 week stay in Long Island, NY at the home office and training location for my new job.

Steve and Barry's, originally called Steve and Barry's University Sportswear, was a new retailer that was popping up in malls and shopping centers all around the United States. Named for Steve Shore and Barry Prevor, the company specialized in collegiate apparel, casual wear, and funny graphic t-shirts. With an average price point of $9.98 or less, their store merchandise was trendy, fun and inexpensive. Through a method of working out deals in dying malls in a few dodgy locations, by 2006 the number of stores was growing rapidly. For less than $20, who wouldn't want their favorite college hoodie and a funny graphic T-shirt?

The company started making headlines when they partnered with professional basketball player Stephon Marbury, who started his Starbury line of sneakers exclusively through their store. Every item in the line, from basketball shoes, to jerseys, was $14.98 or less and it took the country by storm. Mothers would cry in the stores because they could finally afford trendy basketball sneakers for their kids, and instantly Steve and Barry's became a household name. Steve and Barry would take the retail world by storm, showing the power of a price point and celebrity partnerships.

Quickly the store started growing, and growing fast. I can remember someone on TV saying the store was multiplying like rabbits. It was easy to see that taking a ride on this company's train wasn't going to be easy, but it would be exciting. When I saw a cable news channel call the company the "Starbucks of Retail," I embraced that moniker. The next 2 years of my life would be defined by my experiences with the company for better or for worse. The rest of my professional career would be changed forever.

1.

The Cost of Training

One afternoon I was sitting at the car dealership, trying to hide playing a video game on my laptop. Most of my day was spent looking for "ups," which was what we called any customer that walked on our lot. It was far too often that there weren't nearly enough ups for the number of salespeople that worked in our store. I had a lot of down time at that job, and after a few weeks I spent much of my time at work submitting job applications. I doubt there was a restaurant, retail store, or bank with a job opening that I hadn't applied for. I had even applied to work as an actor at one of the stage shows at the nearby amusement park.

One Tuesday morning, I heard my cell phone ring and it was a **recruiter** calling from a company called Steve and Barry's University Sportswear in reference to a job. One of the many applications that I had submitted was to be a store manager at one of their local stores. At that point I had filled out so many applications that if I were to say I was expecting the call it would be as far from the truth as to say I even remember applying. Nonetheless, I pretended to be excited when I answered the phone. I naturally told the recruiter how eagerly I was awaiting hearing from them. As my sales manager taught me, the job of a salesman is to be a good actor, and I was doing my best to win an award.

I had been familiar with Steve and Barry's stores, at least to the point where I had been inside of one of their stores in a mall in Pennsylvania. I had memories of these wood paneled floors that were intentionally designed to look like a basketball court, and these wooden cubes filled with t-shirts that explained where all my friends in college had been doing their shopping. That store also had an abundance of apparel from various Pennsylvania colleges, as well as some other famous colleges. My sense of fashion hadn't ever made it out of the 1980s, so much of the store's appeal was lost on me. What immediately stood out to me was their price-point of $6.98. I had never seen any retailer sell new, branded clothing for a price that low.

On the phone, I heard what sounded like a younger female recruiter with a strong Long Island accent. Her energy and bubbly personality made it impossible not to join in her excitement. She asked me if I was interested in an interview with a district manager. I accepted, for no reason other than that it gave me a chance to get out of the dealership for a few hours. I wasn't entirely sure I even wanted to work there, but I was desperate to put my time as a car salesman behind me.

I interviewed in person a few days later, and it seemed like a relatively standard job interview. I was asked what my biggest achievement in life was, and I quickly explained that I earned my **MBA** while working full time. I thought this would show hard work and dedication. I remember seeing the district manager make a note that I had "an MBA in business" on the application as it was sent off. I didn't feel that I had done well in the interview, but also didn't think I screwed it up too badly either.

A few days later, the same recruiter called to offer me the job as a store manager. She offered me a modest **salary** with a promise of bonus potential. After a few months of scraping by and dealing with the uncertainty of being paid solely on commission, any sort of guaranteed paycheck sounded pretty good. I immediately jumped at the opportunity. She told me all about how the company was growing rapidly, how the launch of a new pair of shoes was going to change the world, and how I'd be a part of it. I realized the recruiter might have been an even better salesperson than I felt I was.

One of the side effects of being raised by my grandparents is I tend to pump the brakes hard when anyone ever seems to be asking me to drink the Kool-Aid. My formative years were also spent listening to far too much stand-up comedy. I question everything. At this point though, I knew that I felt selling cars was an awful way to spend my early 20s, and so was being broke all the time. In the back of my mind, I felt it was possible this was merely propaganda, but maybe it was true. I knew for sure a salaried job with **benefits** seemed attractive. I agreed and was ready to go. Then she described something that should have made me stop and wonder. You know what they say about hindsight being 20/20.

I was no stranger to working full-time or working too many hours in a week. I wasn't new to working in a **retail store**, nor was I new to **retail management**. I had worked in **store management** positions in other once-great companies. I had plenty of different jobs so I felt I knew the standard fare. Show up to work the first day, watch a few videos, sign a few forms, and spend a few days learning how to run a cash register, receive inventory, and count a safe. I prepared myself for the inevitable tax forms and training videos. I wasn't prepared for what I was about to hear.

When the recruiter explained a 2-week trip to Long Island, NY it seemed a little strange. I wasn't sure what 2 weeks of training in the corporate office could offer me, but they said they were paying for my flight, my lodging, and even better, they'd be paying for my meals while I was there. One of my rules on life is that you never turn down a free meal. I wasn't sure what to expect, but the trip sounded interesting. It developed so quickly that I don't remember having any time to think about it, but I packed my bags, booked a taxi to the airport and boarded the plane.

I flew out to New York, knowing absolutely nothing other than I was going to have a roommate named Joe and a trainer named Bailey. I'll admit to not being someone who likes flying very much, but it was my first time flying on someone else's dime and I made it to the hotel in one piece. Maybe it was the idea of New York City, where I had only ever visited before in school organized trips, or maybe I was just ready for something new. I was genuinely excited.

When I arrived at the hotel lobby, I met a few other young people who were there for the same reason I was. As more new recruits arrived at the hotel, I saw that most of them were in their early 20s. All of them had some sort of college degree, some had retail experience, and they all seemed equally eager to get to work. I spent a few hours in the lobby listening to one of the new recruits telling us how she can learn so much about someone's personality by how they sign their name. She told me that the exaggerated large letters in my signature showed I had a larger than life personality and that I loved attention. She definitely hit the nail on the head.

The next morning, we ate breakfast at the hotel and were guided to a convention room to start day one of corporate training. All the recruits were wearing some sort of lanyard name tag, and there were a few easily noticed members of Steve and Barry's corporate office. Unbeknownst to me, the current NYC fashion trend of the times was to wear 2 polo shirts on top of each other, khaki pants, sneakers, and to be constantly staring down at a corporate cell phone. I had never seen an internet equipped phone in action before, but the way they feverishly typed on it, it was a clear sign of importance and seemed a bit of an obsession. Our trainers had the group go through an ice breaker called "two truths and a lie" so we could learn something about each other. I had always thought ice breakers were silly, but I played along.

When I first heard the name Bailey, I was thinking she'd be female. I was surprise when I met him. He wasn't wearing a name tag, but the cell phone attached to his belt was a dead giveaway. Bailey turned out to be an extremely nice, warm, and outwardly excited guy. We all loved him instantly. He sang a lot and let us know how lucky we were to be chosen to train with the company. He would be leading our week of classroom training. He called my roommate "Joey" which he pronounced in an exaggerated New York accent, and got excited when he found out one of my classmate's names was in a famous song because it allowed him to sing her name out loud. Bailey, joined by a tall blonde trainer named Connie, had a way of easing the tension and bringing a level of fun to our long days.

During my first week of classroom training the corporate culture started to sink in. After recently graduating from college, I was likely visibly annoyed at the prospect of sitting in a classroom for 8 hours a day. The rest of the room was as unhappy about it as I was, but we all did our best to fake it. We were all handed binders, pens, and a brown messenger bag to carry around with us. This classroom would be our home for the next week.

Bailey did his best to make this week as fun as he could, as we learned about the history of the company, learned a bit about store operations, and met more people with corporate cell phones. The highlight of week one was when we were taken on a train into NYC where we got to eat at a restaurant on the ground floor of the Empire State Building, and visit a few of our stores in the city. The Empire State Building seems much less exciting when only seeing it from the ground floor, but most of us were still impressed by it.

Most of our meals were given to us in the hotel, usually it was catered food from local chain restaurants. However, for our meals on Thursday and Friday we were told we needed to pay for ourselves and that the company would reimburse us when we returned home from training. As my bank account was depleted, I only had a roll of quarters in my pocket. It was the first time in my life I went over 48 hours without eating. On Saturday when we arrived at the Empire State Building, I grabbed every roll of the table and ate it as fast as I could. I didn't care if anyone else wanted one or not.

We returned to our classroom after visiting the city and were assigned to watch a basketball movie which I've been required to watch multiple times over the years. I don't like basketball, and honestly hated the movie. I asked politely if I could be allowed to go back to my room instead of watching the movie for what felt like the 100th time, but they told me it was important that I stayed in the room with everyone. I begrudgingly agreed, but it was our last day in the classroom together.

The next week we were to transition from staying in a classroom to being trained inside stores. We were going to see actual store operations, as well as the process for opening and closing stores. We saw more corporate cell phones, more dual polo shirts. It was at this point we met both Steve and Barry. To us they were celebrities. We got to see the new Starbury shoes we would all grow to love, or hate. While there were only a few colors available, we could see why they were so popular. They looked like high end shoes, and I could imagine a professional basketball player on the court wearing them.

We were taught how to fold t-shirts, both short and long-sleeved, how to fold pants, how to merchandise and how to work the cash register. Through the week we were given small **visual merchandising** assignments such as setting up displays, dressing mannequins (which makes you feel seriously creepy the first time you do it) and getting to know various **stock keeping units (SKUs)** around the store. We also got to hear a recently released and repetitive pop song every 10 minutes in constant repeat as the video played on the big flat screen TVs around the store. I still hear that song playing in my head.

One night, when we were left on our own for dinner, a few of us went across the street from the hotel to a local arcade style sports bar. I still didn't have any money other than my roll of quarters, but some of my new friends let me use some of their credits to play a few video games. While trying to win a stuffed toy on a trivia game, we all started asking each other what we thought. It seemed that I was not alone in my reservations. We all agreed that since we were getting paid to be in training, we'd stick it out, but that we all felt something rather odd. One recruit told me he planned to quit as soon as he got back home, but would ride out the week of free food. I was a little bit more optimistic, but optimism was never my strong suit.

We finished out the week and we all passed our training. I found out that a handful of the recruits had caused some problems Saturday night upon their return from New York City. My name was clear from any of that debacle. It looked like I had a promising job waiting on me when I flew back home. Maybe if I worked hard enough someday, I'd have a corporate cell phone of my own, but I'd have to face the hard truth of not being able to comfortably fit into 2 polo shirts. One of our recruits was offered a corporate office job during his second week of training, which he quickly accepted. I never knew why he was so quickly offered a promotion, but it made the prospect of a promotion seem more within reach.

When I returned home, I went into the small store that I was assigned to be working at. This store was in a suburb in a small, very old looking shopping center. The neighborhood didn't seem to be a very safe place, and the plaza was in need of a makeover. There were a few stores next to us that looked to have been there for a while. It didn't look very different from the stores in New York, it was just a little smaller.

On my first visit in the store, I walked around trying to pretend I was just another casual shopper. I wanted to get a good look before anyone knew me as a new manager. I was greeted by a few friendly associates who appeared to be happily folding clothes on a table. I got to meet the store director, Tom. I introduced myself and was ready to set my schedule to start working.

I had been hired as a store manager, which in every company I had ever worked for, meant the same as general manager. I had expected to be the highest-ranking member of management in the store. However, it was only after arriving at my corporate training that I found out I was a store manager, which is what in any other company I had every worked for would call an "assistant" manager. Tom was store "director," meaning it was Tom who would be in charge of the store. I would report to Tom, along with two other store managers. I was a bit disappointed, but felt like some of the pressure was lifted off my shoulders.

Tom was a really nice guy, and was one of my favorite people I would ever work with. He was a fan of professional football and told me he had a degree in history. When I told him I was a bit of a World War 2 buff, he recommended some books for me to read. Despite the blow to my massive ego about not being in charge myself, I looked forward to working with him. Tom took me out to lunch and we had a longer conversation about how things would work in our store.

"I'm going to have to get you up to speed quickly and train you on how to work here" he told me.

"Oh, I learned all about that in New York. You can hand me the keys and I'm ready to go" I foolishly replied.

"Sorry man, but the corporate office is months behind, and most of what they taught you is probably is already outdated. The rest of what they taught you is just wrong."

Tom wasn't wrong. Next to nothing that I had learned about store operations in the last 2 weeks of training had any relation to what the job actually looked like. Absolutely none of the procedures we were taught there were currently in use. I had a sudden feeling my training had been smoke and mirrors. I knew my real training was to happen in the store. I walked away wondering how much the 2 weeks on Long Island cost the company for all of us in my training class. I never did calculate it.

Chapter 1 Key Terms

1. Benefits
2. MBA
3. Recruiter
4. Retail
5. Retail Management
6. Salary
7. Shopping center
8. stock keeping unit (SKU)
9. Store management
10. Trend (trendy)
11. Visual merchandising

Chapter Takeaways

- Recruiting retail managers can be difficult, as potential applicants can have a wide range of education and experience.
- Companies need to be upfront and honest about the expectations of the job.
- Management training is of vital importance to an organization, but must be done in a cost-effective manner.

Discussion Questions

1. What were some reasons the author felt "odd" during his training with the company? How do you think you would feel in this situation?
2. The author implied the training for the company seemed to be ineffective. Why did he feel this way? What could the company have done to make it more effective?
3. The author implied the cost of training was higher than necessary. How could the company have decreased training costs while still being effective?
4. This chapter shows some examples of the company culture. How would you describe the culture of this company?

2.

Celebrity Endorsements

After learning how to use the SOC (only corporate employees called it the "sock," store managers called it the "S-O-C"), our **intranet system** for store communications, things felt like they were finally coming together. My expensive corporate training might not have taught me everything I needed to know, but I was quickly learning a lot in the store. The **hourly employees** seemed to like me, and things started feeling relatively comfortable. Our store was one of the older and smaller stores in the company, but we had our store running like a well-oiled machine. Tom, as well as the other two store managers, had been a strong team and I was glad to be part of it. I didn't exactly feel like I fit in right away, but they were kind and welcoming to the new guy.

Basketball star Stephon Marbury had helped to start a transformation that would take a small t-shirt store and put it at the center of the competitive retail world. Previously, we had sold mostly collegiate apparel for college-age males, and in the company's history never sold any of their merchandise for more than $9.98. The company had become successful by **targeting** college students and mostly younger males through a low-price **strategy**. The company had never utilized any **celebrity endorsements**.

Steve and Barry's had a **price point** under discount stores low price retailers, but it took a pair of sneakers and a basketball player from Coney Island to get the whole world to pay attention to us. Stephon had teamed up with our company to launch his **product line** of shoes, appropriately called Starbury. They looked like high priced basketball shoes, but had a **target market** with a more modest income. The original shoe was a high-top shoe that Stephon wore on the court. I thought the shoes were ugly, but I could tell they were absolutely in line with current shoe fashion.

Unlike other big-name professional basketball stars who sold shoes with bigger shoe brands, Starbury shoes would only sell for $14.98 a pair. These shoes were not only trendy, they were affordable. Kids from lower income families were wearing them, parents were loving them, and customers were buying them out of our stores. Our store couldn't ever keep the original Starbury shoes in stock. Popular sizes sold out immediately, and Stephon became an in-house celebrity.

I hadn't worn high top sneakers since I was in middle school, but once the Starbury line started making more casual sneakers, I bought a few pairs. I was impressed. They were comfortable, and felt nothing like what the low price made me think they would feel like. I could see why these shoes were so popular. Stephon's picture was everywhere in our store, and, along with another basketball star "Big" Ben Wallace. Their presence dominated the store layout. We even had a Starbury team member who came in our store and was able to spin a basketball off a pencil that he stuck in his shoelaces. I loved watching what he could do with a basketball.

Stephon's popularity was soaring, and the company quickly sought to copy the model into other lines to reach other **demographics**. The next celebrity line came from Sarah Jessica Parker, an actress best known for her leading role as a 30-something, fashion conscious, successful New York woman. To me she was always the witch in that Halloween movie. She had popularized the cosmopolitan cocktail, and her influence on women was worth a lot.

Sarah would move to introduce a product line of clothing for women called Bitten. She chose the name because of when she started doing live theater she felt "bitten" by the theater bug. Her line was a highly fashionable women's line, similar to something her TV character would wear. The entire line had a **price ceiling** of $19.98.

With her line came a drastic change in our **store layout**. We would split our store down the middle, with Starbury on the right and Bitten on the left. If our stores looked like a basketball court before, they looked like a trendy, modern clothing store now. We all felt this was a much-needed facelift and our stores felt fresh and seemed happy.

The other store employees and I were stunned when our small store was chosen as one of the prized stops on Stephon Marbury's "Starbury Tour." The plan for the tour would include making appearances in stores to greet excited fans and shoppers. We knew this stop in the tour would bring us more **media exposure** than we had ever experienced and get our store on the map. Steve and Barry's had well over 200 locations at this point, so it was easy for our little store to be overshadowed. This was the first time we felt our hard work would pay off.

Stephon's tour would hit a number of stores across the country. His tour would travel in two oversized limousines, one for Stephon and one for his entourage. We didn't know if this was by Stephon's request or if it was our company's way of trying to be noticed. I had, at first, felt it was a little ridiculous but it was certainly a sight to see.

In the weeks leading up to the tour, we were well prepared, well stocked and were given permission to schedule extra employees to get the store in perfect shape. We were told when he came there would be a number of TV cameras and we were to look our best. This was our store's best chance to succeed and we weren't going to blow it. We all knew this was a huge opportunity.

Stephon was scheduled to arrive at our store in the mid-afternoon, and a few hours earlier we already had customers in our store waiting for him. We had seen videos of mothers crying and thanking him for his shoes, and the swarms of fans looking to get his autograph on a pair of shoes or a basketball. I had never seen our store that clean or organized before, nor had I ever seen our store so busy. Our stock of Starbury apparel was extra full. Naturally, I was not surprised when about an hour before his scheduled arrival I received a phone call from the corporate office. I was, however, stunned by the nature of the call.

"We need you to remove the Bitten products from any visible area in the front of the store and move it to the back of the store." As soon as I was able to speak I asked for clarification.

"What do you mean, move all of her clothing?" I uttered. The corporate employee then told me that Stephon was upset that during his previous stop he felt the Bitten products were overshadowing Starbury. They told us Stephon would only be in the front part of our store, and that he would leave if he saw any of her merchandise next to his.

"We can't just move some shirts, we would have to move entire displays, change signs, and rearrange half the store," I said in desperation. My cries were quickly cut off.

"And that needs to be done before he gets to your store or he's not walking inside. Make sure that happens."

Luckily for us he showed up a few hours late, buying us time to complete the seemingly impossible rearrangement. We were told he had been hungry for lunch and had stopped at a casual restaurant chain located on the other side of the city. Our hastily performed store layout change didn't look quite as sharp as it had before, but every instance of the Sarah Jessica Parker's line was hidden in the back of the store. From the camera eye only Stephon and Ben Wallace could be seen from the front. There was Starbury in every direction.

Shortly after, the giant limousines pulled up. A **handler**, a college-aged female, came in our store and gave us a list of Starbury apparel we need to give them for Stephon to wear. I was rather confused, as I didn't know what she meant.

"What do you mean give him clothing? Are you telling me he didn't bring any of his own apparel with him?" I asked. We were then told that he would only wear Starbury clothing we provided for him. We quickly supplied them with a full wardrobe, and waited for him to come in the store.

As expected, a line of customers smiled, cried and asked for autographs. The local news captured it all, and Stephon told them about how maybe someday the biggest basketball stars would follow in his footsteps. He explained that someday maybe we will see his shoes combined with bigger brands in stores across America. While I was certainly hoping that was simply his dry sense of humor, he did mention to us privately how Sarah Jessica Parker needed to stop riding his coattails. We all had a laugh, and a sigh of relief when the event was over.

Before long, more celebrity lines were popping up around our store. Amanda Bynes launched her "Dear" line for teenage girls, Bubba Watson had golfing polos, and even Venus Williams and Laird Hamilton had jumped on board with their own lines of athletic clothing. None of these lines ever blossomed like Bitten and Starbury, but they were a welcome addition to our store.

Shortly after we received a call from corporate saying we weren't allowed to talk about Stephon if the media were to ask us anything. Come to find out, the company believed some of his most recent media interviews had alluded to a few things they didn't want our customers to read. We didn't need any bad press so we were all told to direct any inquiries from the media to the corporate office. No media inquiries ever came, and we never heard of the interview again.

Chapter 2 Key Terms

1. Celebrity endorsement
2. Demographics
3. Handler
4. Hourly employee
5. Intranet
6. Media Exposure
7. Price ceiling
8. Price point
9. Price strategy
10. Product line
11. Store layout
12. Target market
13. Targeting

Chapter Takeaways

- Celebrity endorsements and product lines can be successful ways of reaching new customers.
- Celebrities can be difficult to deal with and in-store events can be problematic.
- Celebrity product lines can be wildly successful, but they aren't easy to replicate.
- Too much focus on celebrity lines can cause a company's image to shift and the success of a company can become too dependent on the popularity and public opinion of the celebrity.

Discussion Questions

1. Steve and Barry's grew in popularity with the introduction of the Starbury line. In what ways did this line help grow the business?
2. Celebrity lines allowed the company to reach new audiences. How was this possible?
3. The celebrity lines were still sold for a low price, but at a higher price than the store had previously sold products. Do you think the price of these lines was appropriate? Explain your answer.
4. In what ways can a celebrity endorsement be difficult for a company? Do you think the benefits outweighed the difficulties? Explain your answer.

Visual Audits

A fast-food breakfast sandwich always helped my drive to work. I had a relatively long commute to work, but aside from breakfast calories and an oversized cup of coffee there was a local FM radio station with a mildly entertaining morning show. The show hosts helped lighten my mood and I always enjoyed listening to their program. I worked in radio long enough that I normally don't like morning shows, but I always liked feeling they were awake as early as I was.

In retail, things were cyclical, repeatable and predictable. My days had so many routines that I felt like I woke up to the same day every morning. When I worked the morning shift, I would pull up to the store an hour before opening. I would usually be greeted by one of my hourly employees waiting on me. One cashier in particular, Katelyn, would always be taking slow drags off her morning menthol cigarette while I pulled into the parking lot. While I always like to be 15 minutes early for everything, I tried to never show up earlier to work than need be.

Our store had a rather smart policy that not even managers were allowed to enter the store alone. This was to protect our employees from being robbed while they were alone, and also protected the company from managers stealing anything from the store when no one else was looking. This buddy system always helped. Katelyn never minded waiting for me as she always enjoyed some time with her menthol cigarette. I enjoyed eating my breakfast and drinking my coffee.

The first in the list of **store opening procedures** included opening the front door, locking it behind me, and turning on only the lights in the back of the store. It was never a good idea to make the store look open before it was, as we didn't want to attract any customers before we needed to. We always made sure to keep the front of the store as dark and lifeless as possible before opening. Most of the Steve and Barry's locations were inside a mall, so the only early arrivals were senior mall walkers. We hoped that if we kept the lights off, they'd just keep on walking instead of coming in and knocking on the front door.

However, the rest of the morning routine was simply that, routine. Cashiers needed drawers, clothing needed to be put out on the floor, and you needed to spend at least 5 minutes grumbling about the employees last night who never seemed to do a good job of closing the store. Managers in the morning always have a way of saying last night's employees missed something, and the store was never up to their high standards. The trick was making sure, before you complained, it wasn't you who closed the night before. If so, the conversation would quickly move to how busy you were the night before and how there would have been no possible way to have properly cleaned or closed the store. You convinced yourself that your **closing shifts** were always too busy, and everyone else should have done so much more during their shifts.

The real problem with opening a retail store is that, despite arriving an hour before the store opening, you rarely ever had time to get the store opened in time. Not to mention, you probably were there the night before and were wondering why you didn't just sleep in the office. There are always too many reports to fill out, too many items to get on the floor, or too many displays to **stage**. For us, this was just par for the course. Things in retail are always done **just-in-time**, and if you had "time to lean you had time to clean." In retail, you always made sure you never had time to lean.

I'll never forget the first time my morning routine was interrupted by what every store manager in the company feared more than anything.

We had a Pavlovian reaction every single time the phone rang before the store opened. Most of the time it was simply a customer asking what time we opened, or if you had a specific pair of Starbury shoes in their size available in the store. The problem was when the phone conversation sounded more like this.

"Good morning, Steve and Barry's. How may I help you?"

"Good morning, this is Frank calling you from the corporate office to inform you that today we are having a visual audit. You need to take the following 10 photos and have them submitted before the store opens." The calls always came from a division of the corporate office that none of us had any direct contact with. We were never given more than the first name of the caller.

When I would hear the words **visual audit,** no amount of coffee was going to save my morning. Instead of proceeding with my regular morning routine, I would have to scramble to complete this audit and turn it in before the store opened. I knew that a failed visual audit would result in reprimand, so I always worked to get them in on time and score as high as I could.

A visual audit was a requirement in our store that happened on random days. We were never given any warning, just a phone call from corporate sometime before the store was opened. We would be given specific points in the store, usually 10 or so, that would be audited that day. One day it might be the men's **department**, or a table of denim, or shoes, and another day it might be certain displays of dressed mannequins or maybe even the stockroom. We would have to very quickly grab the digital camera out of the safe and take those specific photos and send them to the corporate office. They would then grade us on these photos. The closer our photos matched the intended design in the SOC, the higher our grade would be.

Before Steve and Barry's grew into the larger operation that it would eventually become, it was once a small store operated solely between two friends named Steve Shore and Barry Prevor. During our training they told us that the two friends flipped a coin for whose name would appear first. Barry won that toss, but the similarity to a famous brand of ice cream convinced them to use Steve's name first.

Steve was, from my perspective, a dedicated and talented entre-preneur. In the early days of the company, we were told Steve liked to travel to the stores himself and see first-hand the company he had built. However, it was explained to us that Steve hated to fly and once the company started becoming scattered across the country, he had to relinquish the idea of seeing his operations in person. A visual audit was his way of seeing inside his stores. He would know if his stores were clean, well-stocked, or not up to standards.

My salary never felt like it was nearly enough, but no salary ever does. The perk to my salary was that it did include an attractive **bonus structure**, which often made a sizable increase to my **take-home pay**. One of the ways we could receive a bonus was on our score on the visual audits. The company took them very seriously. It always made sense to me that the company would want to see what was happening in their stores, but I certainly felt there had to have been a better way than rushing to upload photographs to a department across the globe.

The big challenge we had in our audit was not due to our ability to keep our store clean and organized but due to being in a small store. We were never one of the company's priority stores. As a young operation, they couldn't always get all the product to all of the stores. The bigger stores took precedence. We simply learned that sometimes other stores would get merchandise we wouldn't get, so we tried not to let it bother us. The problem was, we often didn't get items required on our audits.

"What do you mean I lost points for the men's department? Everything in that room was folded, displayed and in the right place. You're costing me money, man" I would shout at the phone.

It would be explained to me that there were polo shirts on manne-quins we were supposed to have, or a style of jeans that should have been on a table. I'd be told that I'd lose points on the audit, and subse-quently part of my bonus, because of the missing items.

I'd do my best to beg, plead, and at times, yell and argue. "Look, we are in a small store. I can't put that new polo on the mannequin if my store didn't receive any." Inevitably, I'd be told over the phone that it was their job to rate my photo by what the company told them to rate it by. If they were told our store was supposed to have something, then we were supposed to have it. If they were told something was supposed to be in the photo, then it was supposed to be in the photo. No amount of "we don't even have that" mattered. As far as I was concerned, no amount of my bonus check seemed to matter to them either.

To this day I don't like digital cameras. I often wonder why I don't have one single photo of myself from when I worked there. I don't have a picture of myself from my training in New York, nor do I have a photo of first day of work there. I guess I still feel every time I take a photo of myself that someone is going to tell me I'm losing points, losing money, or that I don't have on what I'm supposed to have on.

Chapter 3 Key Terms

1. Bonus structure
2. Closing shift
3. Department
4. Just-in-time
5. Stage
6. Store opening procedures
7. Take-home-pay
8. Visual audit

Chapter Takeaways

- An employee's compensation can often be impacted by a bonus, but it should be determined by performance that is possible for the employee.
- Visual merchandising is an important part of any store and should be taken seriously by a company.
- The company utilized visual audits to rate the visual appearance of its stores.
- Retail managers' jobs are driven by routines, and disruption to that routine can be frustrating.

Discussion Questions

1. The author mentioned that a career in retail can be full of routines. What were some of his daily routines?
2. The author made the case that visual audits were unfair and a burden on employees. Do you agree? Why or why not? Explain your answer.
3. The company found the visual audits to be very important. What other ways could they have determined the visual appearance of their stores?
4. Retail managers place a lot of emphasis on their bonus. Other than a visual audit, what could have been other factors to determine their bonuses?

Loss Prevention

"Nothing is worse than a thief," my grandmother used to tell me. My grandparents grew up depression era-farmers in small towns in Pennsylvania. My grandfather spent 30 years in the Marine Corps and was always a very intimidating man. He was the type who you could see yelling at recruits in boot camp. He would tell you not to salute him. He'd say "he works for a living." The stories of his military days were family legend, as he was notorious for being the toughest guy you could ever meet. He also had a long career as an electrical engineer for which he was given early retirement when the local plant closed. He taught me to work for everything, ask for nothing, but certainly to never steal anything from someone else.

It should come to no surprise that **shoplifters** are a group of people that I typically don't like. I remember thinking that maybe if we sold baby formula, or food, or something that would give cause to **shoplifting** then I could at least understand, if not condone their actions. What I couldn't understand was stealing **costume jewelry** or low-priced clothing. I didn't think getting caught stealing a $3 pair of earrings made a lot of logical sense. I figured the reward was hardly worth the risk, and even a bored teenager could find something else to do. I also felt that shoplifting in our store would be rare, but I couldn't have been further from the truth. The sheer number of shoplifters we would have come into our stores made me think there was a criminal empire of costume jewelry thieves and an underground network of college hoodie wearing criminals.

Every employee learned a lot about how to spot a shoplifter. They'd come in every size, shape, and color. We learned there were some obvious signs. We would watch for anyone who walked into the store pushing a stroller without a baby, but with plenty of room for merchandise. We soon learned that was as much of a clue as a large jacket in the middle of summer, a flat-bottomed purse, or someone who always seems to be looking at the ceiling trying to find where the security cameras were located. Spotting a shoplifter became a bit of a work of art, and a job we enjoyed doing.

We learned that great customer service was the best way to stop a thief. Most petty thieves wouldn't steal anything if an employee was watching. Great employees are a great deterrent to theft. Our employees often gave the best service to the customers we knew were planning to steal something. It became a sort of game to all of us.

We practiced the SMILE method of customer service. This stood for: Say hi, Make eye contact, Inform the customer, Let them shop, and Express appreciation. It helped us help customers, taught us when to leave customers alone, and how to make customers feel welcome in our stores. It also helped us keep our eye on anyone trying to walk out the front door with anything they didn't pay for.

The sheer volume of shoplifting that happened in our store was more than any amount of great store employees could handle, and **loss prevention** became an important focus. This warranted a strong group of **loss prevention associates**. An entire division of our company, like most retail companies, was dedicated to loss prevention, which would later be changed to a more euphemistic title of "**asset protection**."

In our stores, it was their job to not only prevent theft, but to also apprehend shoplifters and file police reports. These loss prevention employees worked for their own division within the company, but physically worked in our stores. It was their job to walk around like a shopper. They dressed like shoppers, acted like shoppers, and tried to blend in. Then they would call the police and we would watch the shoplifter leave in handcuffs.

Our loss prevention, or "LP" employees, as they called themselves, had very strict rules they had to follow to be able to approach a shoplifter. They had to visually see the person select and conceal the merchandise. They weren't allowed to lose eye contact with the shoplifter after they had concealed the merchandise. They also had to witness the shoplifter pass the last **point of sale**, and fully commit to leaving the store without paying. They were also never allowed to apprehend a customer outside the store, which was a rule in place to protect the employee from any weapons or any armed accomplices.

The job of our LP associates was not an easy one. There were times we all wished our job was to walk around instead of what we considered actually working, but understanding the danger the LP employees could potentially face made folding t-shirts for 8 hours on a Friday evening sound much more appealing. Their job was dangerous, exciting, boring, and certainly unpredictable. All of us in the stores rallied behind our LP employees, and we always silently (or sometimes, not so silently) cheered them on when they'd apprehend someone. A good LP associate would apprehend someone at least daily.

One employee I worked with, Jeb, was a tall, shorthaired southern guy in his 20s who often wore expensive pairs of designer jeans. Jeb was a master at spotting a shoplifter. When he saw one, he'd give me a nod, or sometimes a few clicks on my walkie-talkie to let me know that he had someone in the store who had just pocketed something. Then it was game on. Everyone in the store was quickly alerted to try to act normally, but to watch what was about to happen. We knew Jeb was going to catch them, we knew he'd apprehend them, and we knew they'd go to jail.

As soon as they would pass the last point of sale, Jeb would casually walk up, flash his badge, and tell the shoplifter they were caught and needed to come back to the back office. Reluctantly and red-faced, they'd always follow. I'm not sure why I never saw anyone run after getting caught, but it was probably because they confused his badge for one from the police. It was my job to simply accompany them to the office and wait for the police to arrive.

"How much money do you have in your pocket?" the police officer would always start by asking.

"None at all," was almost always their reply.

"So, you left your house without money and came in the store. So you came here planning to steal."

This line would get them every single time, and make conviction much easier for everyone involved. Then the officer would look at all of the merchandise they stole. It was rarely more than $50 worth. Teenage girls would typically be caught with a pocketful of earrings, the rest would normally have a pair of shoes or a sweatshirt that amounted to what could be bought for $25. I always wondered how much jail time any of them did. I never followed up with the local courts to find out.

Another LP employee I worked with was much sneakier about how he would apprehend a shoplifter. On more than a few occasions he would ask me to not assist, but be within eyesight of him just to make sure his apprehensions went as planned. He had a few ways of catching a thief that I had never heard of before.

"There's a customer out there who just pocketed a few pairs of shoes, but I wasn't able to watch them the whole time, so I'm technically not allowed to approach them. Thing is, I know they stole the shoes, and I'm completely sure they still have them. I need you to stand in front of the store and maybe pretend to smoke a cigarette and just keep your eye on me, OK?"

By that point, the customer had left the store and gone out into the parking lot. I knew why he wanted me to keep him in his sights, as approaching a thief in the parking lot could mean personal danger to my associate, but I had no idea what he was planning to do. He reached in his wallet and pulled out some cash.

"Hey, I'll give you $50 for the shoes you just took? Yeah, that'll save me money inside the store, and it's $50 for you" he told the customer. As soon as she showed him the shoes, he flashed his badge and told her he worked for the store and was going to be calling the police. Instead of getting in her car and driving away, she reluctantly listened to him and followed him inside to wait on the police.

As she walked inside, he pointed up at the ceiling above the door and said "See that?" making her look up at the door. "I hope you just smiled pretty, because we now have your face on camera. Now you'll know never to shoplift again."

I tried hard not to laugh, because I didn't want the shoplifter to know there was no camera above the doorway. I just let him do his job and let one more shoplifter leave my store in handcuffs. While shoplifting might not land someone with a heavy prison sentence, I figured they likely wouldn't steal from my store again if they thought we had their picture at our store on a wall of shame somewhere in the office.

Despite the number of shoplifters we caught, no amount of **external theft** could account for **shrinkage** that we could have from our **internal theft**. While I had only ever thought of it as **pilfering** a few pens, I would soon learn how much employees could successfully take from our stores.

In one of my favorite initiatives, the company had an **employee incentive** for catching internal theft. They understood that our stores were made up mostly of minimum wage hourly employees who were students in high school. They would likely not turn in another employee for stealing. To get their cooperation we offered a reward of $500, or 10% of the value of the theft (whichever is higher) to the employee who turned them in. We always told new employees this during their training, and it happened every so often that an employee would steal a pair of shoes on their first day. One of my seasoned employees would immediately make a $500 phone call. The $500 was more than they would make that week working in the store.

Some employees in another store were rumored to have brought about elaborate schemes to steal merchandise. I heard once that two employees in another store would text each other the whereabouts of the manager so that they could pocket some merchandise. This scheme was eventually totaled at over $30,000, giving a $3000 prize to the employee who alerted the company.

Younger employees often gave their friends their discounts, or simply gave away a free shirt or pair of pants when their friends would shop in the store. This was called "**free-bagging**." The first time one of our employees was fired, and arrested, for stealing clothes from the store I was in a mild state of shock. I had never seen an employee leave a store in handcuffs before and have to take a walk of shame across the sales floor in plain sight of other employees.

One of the ways employees would get charged with internal theft was not theft of merchandise, but **time theft**. It was possible to actually steal time. The thought process behind being terminated for time theft was that employees would put themselves "on the clock," while they weren't working. They would clock in a friend, clock in an hour after they finished working, or much earlier than they arrived. Anytime an employee was caught, the interrogation interview went all the same.

"Have you stolen time from the company?" a corporate LP associate might ask.

"No, of course not, I'm always honest about when I'm at work."

Looking to close the deal, you'd inevitably hear next "So, when you come to work, have you ever clocked in before you took your coat off and put it in your locker." This would always lead to them agreeing, which would then be followed by saying "so you do this every day? Five days a week? For 2 years." This always ended with a now former employee leaving our store in tears.

"Cha-ching," we'd always hear our LP associates say after someone was apprehended. They were incentivized to catch shoplifters. I never knew if they were paid a commission or simply given a quota to meet, but they were in constant competition with each other. Internal theft must have counted for double, or at least gave them some added bragging rights. Every LP associate I worked with knew their value to the company was rated entirely in how many shoplifters they caught or employees they turned in.

Chapter 4 Key Terms

1. Costume jewelry
2. Employee incentive
3. External theft
4. Internal theft
5. Loss prevention

6. Loss prevention employee
7. Pilfering
8. Point of sale (POS)
9. Shoplifter/shoplifting
10. Shrinkage
11. Time

Chapter Takeaways

- Loss prevention is a necessary, and sometimes dangerous task.
- While shoplifting can account for loss, internal theft is the biggest threat.
- Great customer service can be a great deterrent to theft.
- Time theft is a type of internal theft that can be common among hourly employees.

Discussion Questions

1. What were the requirements for a loss prevention associate to confront a shoplifter? What could be the challenges of following these steps?
2. Employees were taught to try to spot shoplifters. What were some of the behaviors an employee would look for? What could be some other behaviors that could seem suspicious?
3. Do you think the employee reward program for turning in other employees for theft was a useful program? Would this program convince you to turn in a fellow associate?
4. What were some of the ways that employees could commit internal theft? Other than the incentive program, what are some other ways a manager could reduce internal theft among employees?

5.

Armed Robbery

Shoplifters might have been a constant nuisance, but at least in the stores I managed no one was ever physically hurt by someone simply stealing a t-shirt. None of our employees were ever attacked or harmed. Shoplifting happened a lot, and most of us were desensitized to it. No amount of training ever prepared us for when we were being robbed at gun-point. None of us ever thought it would ever happen to our little store.

During training, every associate at every retail store I have ever worked at was taught procedures for **retail security** and how to handle an armed robber. It's sort of like when your teachers told you what to do in the event of a fire. We all know the drill, but none of us ever expect to see it happen in-person. We tell ourselves how we are going to handle it, and what we are going to do, but until it happens, none of us are ever prepared for it. We were told to stay calm, do exactly as we're told, and just give them whatever it is they're asking for. Our job was not worth the risk, regardless of how much cash is in the register.

In all my years in retail leading up to this point, I had envisioned exactly how I would handle a robbery. I always thought of the famous scene in a famous movie from the 1980s where a character was held up at gunpoint. He courageously throws a hot pot of coffee in the assailant's face. Unfortunately, most of us aren't that brave or that stupid, and we rarely have a piping hot weapon at our disposal. Not to mention, we are all explicitly told not to ever even consider doing this.

When we're told not to panic during training, we didn't realize how hard that is. Airlines announce to flyers to panic when they start descending rapidly nose pointed toward the ground. We were supposed to walk slowly and not make any sudden movements. We were supposed to open and empty the cash registers. We shouldn't move toward a **panic button**. While our store had panic buttons installed, they were disabled so that no employee would ever use one. We were taught not to yell and not to alert anyone. We were to cooperate and remain calm.

Once in our store we saw a customer who many of us thought was acting rather odd, but left without incident. The next day we found out that shortly after he left, the store next door was robbed and the employees were all made to lay on the ground while the criminals emptied the safe and left. We all sent our condolences to those employees and we all hoped they were okay. That time we were lucky we scared off the assailants without even knowing it. We never knew what we did to avoid that situation, but we were thankful.

A safety measure that we had in our store was a code word. Cashiers can't open the cash registers themselves without some sort of manager or head cashier override, nor can they get into the office to open a safe. For those, they'd need to call a manager for help. The problem was, if you call a manager to ask for help giving money to a robber, you ran the risk of scaring them and making their trigger finger happier than you'd like. Our code was designed to not lead them onto anything.

All our employees were well trained in our code words. The corporate office did have a separate code word for the security system, one that we would tell the **alarm services company** if the **security alarm** was set off by accident or if it was a break-in. While every manager had an **individual alarm code**, there was a universal password if the alarm was tripped. When I set our alarm off by accident one morning, I didn't know that the password was "avocado." I was supposed to have learned that during training, but it must have slipped my mind. After having to explain to the police it was my mistake, I never made the mistake again.

We sold a lot of t-shirts, and all of them were folded before being stored in cubes. We had these blue boards that would help us fold t-shirts, but even with help, the t-shirt rooms always seemed the most Sisyphean task we had. Sometimes I'd find myself folding for hours and not feeling like I'd even made a dent in getting the room in order. It was easy to become completely lost in time in a room full of t-shirts.

One evening, after an hour of t-shirt folding, I heard something come across my walkie-talkie that I had never heard before. "I need Steve or Barry to come to the front register" I looked up from a sea of shirts, and stared blankly forward for what felt like an eternity. I second guessed that I had heard the code for armed robbery. I thought for a second before saying another word.

"I'm in the t-shirt room, did you need something?" I replied.

"Yes, I need Steve or Barry to come to the front registers." My cashier said again.

From my vantage point I couldn't see to the front of the store, but now I knew I wasn't imagining what I had heard. "Steve and Barry" was the code red, shields up code that I never thought I'd hear. We were being robbed. I immediately turned the corner to the front of the store and saw two of my cashiers standing in front of their registers with the cash registers wide open. The younger of the two looked like a deer in headlights. The other, a head cashier named Anne, quickly told me what happened.

"Yeah, he waved his gun at me and said to open the drawers and give us his money. He took the money, ran out front and jumped in the car and turned the corner fast. It all happened in what seemed like 10 seconds."

"Are you ok?" I stupidly asked.

"Hun, I'm from around here. Do you really think that was the first time someone has ever waved a gun in my face?" To this day I'm glad it was Anne there that day. Anne handled it better than I ever could, and was almost completely unaffected by it. I'm not sure I would have been able to even speak afterwards had it happened to me.

Being what I thought was a responsible manager, I picked up the phone and immediately called to report the incident. "We were just robbed at gun point. I assumed you were the first person I'm supposed to call." I said to my district manager.

"Did you seriously call me before calling the police? Hang up and call the police." She quickly said to me. In hindsight, that seems to be what made more sense. Guns and robberies tend to push the common sense right out of someone.

When the police arrived, they told us to let all the customers leave and they closed the store. We explained what happened, and they asked Anne for a description and took some notes on one of those little pads of paper cops always seem to have in their pocket.

"Let's go back to the office and watch the security tape and we will see what we can do" was his first step. Unfortunately, I then explained to them that, other than the alarm for the doors, our company didn't have any other **physical security systems**, and there weren't any cameras anywhere in the store, "Well, sounds to me like you're SOL." That was about the only consolation we received that day from the police.

We never did get a camera system installed in the store, but the company hired a security team to stand near the store exit for a couple of weeks. A national security company was chosen to provide us with a guard whose job was to stand at the front of the store as a deterrent to these sorts of incidents. I'll never forget the agent we received. She was probably 5 feet tall, collecting social security, and told us how she was afraid of the rain. I just hoped she wasn't afraid of shoplifters.

During this time, I had been splitting my time between my smaller home store and an oversized new store in the city. This new store was extremely large and free standing. It had previously been a large major retailer, but had been an empty building for a long time. The sheer size of this store was daunting to say the least, but there were a large number of problems with the store from the beginning. They had gone through multiple management teams before the store had even opened. It seemed to be a store that was destined for problems.

The store was most often one of the top 10 in sales in the entire company. The economy was growing and the company was growing even faster. The Steve and Barry's experience was catching on. I began working at that store on occasion when another manager was on vacation, but my time at that store started becoming more frequent. I had quickly become a popular manager among the staff of that store. While I'd love to tell myself they liked me because I was a great manager, I really think they were just happy to see a familiar face after all the changes they'd gone through.

I received a call one night from my district manager telling me of a robbery that happened at this bigger store as well. They had been robbed at gun point, the employees were freaked out and the company was going to transfer me to that store permanently. I was told that it would prove to be a huge opportunity at this store, and they felt they were more comfortable with me being the new manager there after the robbery. I always assumed they meant that I was their chosen employee to be shot if it was going to happen.

As soon as I arrived at the new store the next day, I received a warm welcome from the employees. They were very happy to see me, and many of them couldn't wait to pull me aside and tell me their thoughts in private. In their own words, they all told me someone came into the store close to closing time with a gun and made all the cashiers give them money. He had robbed the store at such a time that he was able to leave with a good amount of cash. The way it happened seemed odd to everyone in the store.

One of my favorite stockroom employees, Neil, told me bluntly his thoughts. "I think it was an inside job. The new cashier we hired seemed really weird last night, and I think he was in on it." He truly felt this new employee was up to no good. This time, instead of calling my district manager with the news, I called the police and asked to speak to the detective on the case. A few days later a detective called me back.

"Is there a way you can get me inside your office without employees seeing me enter the store? Can I just come in the back door or something?" the detective asked me.

I explained that we had a back door for **receiving** and I'd let him in. He told me that they had already gotten other reports of evidence that this employee had been responsible for the robbery and said they want to bring him in for questioning. I explained that this employee was working right now out on the floor. I was instructed to go out and get him, bring him in the office, but to make something up and not to tell him why he was really coming back office. I said I would mention something with our **cash handling procedures**.

"Hey, remember when we **counted up** your drawer today? Oh man, sorry there's this new form we are supposed to fill out and we didn't fill it out. Could you come back to the office and do that now? Thanks!" I lied. I didn't feel bad about it either.

Upon entering the back office, the detective stood up. He had that classic look of detectives I had seen on TV. He was wearing a sport jacket with no tie due to the size of his neck. He had these giant ham hocks for hands, and when he shook your hand, you felt the bones in your fingers crackling. He walked up to the surprised employee, shook his hand as hard as he could, looked him dead in the eye.

"I know you did it. Don't lie to me, I can see it in your eyes. I can smell the guilt on you from here so whatever you do don't lie to me and tell me you didn't do it."

"I didn't have anything to do with the robbery" the employee quickly muttered.

"I wasn't talking about the robbery, but I'm glad you brought it up."

A few minutes later he could have gotten anyone to admit to just about anything he wanted. The detective brought him with him to the station for questioning, but told us to leave him on the clock.

"Keep him on the clock so he knows it's voluntary. Don't worry, he's going to fess up to it. I'll call you as soon as he does. Then you can clock him out and fire him."

I normally don't like firing people, but I really don't like my employees having guns waved at them. That day was one of the rare times I felt I had seen something good happen. The good guys won. I remember telling my head stockroom employee how happy I was that he had helped get that kid caught.

I choose to remember Neil for that time he helped catch a thief. I remember how much he helped us with the police investigation, and how it only ever happened because he trusted me enough to tell me what he thought might have happened. I try to forget when, weeks later, he was fired for time theft.

Chapter 5 Key Terms

1. Alarm services company
2. Cash handling procedures
3. Code word
4. Counting up (drawer)
5. Individual alarm code
6. Panic button
7. Physical security system
8. Receiving (location)
9. Retail security
10. Security alarm

Chapter Takeaways

- Working in retail can put employees and managers at risk for physical harm from armed robberies.
- Handling an armed robbery can be a frightening experience and it is difficult to remember the procedures when it is happening.
- Physical security systems, especially camera systems, are important investments in retail. When there is no video evidence of a robbery it makes it difficult for police to investigate.
- While less common, internal theft can include employees arranging for armed robberies.

Discussion Questions

1. What were the procedures employees were instructed to follow during a robbery? Do you think you could follow these procedures if you were at gun-point?
2. The author mentions some of the code words that were in use at the store. What were these and how were they used?

3. How did the manager and detective work to identify the employee who was responsible? Do you agree with the tactics used? Why or why not?

4. The author identifies a camera as a type of security system that the company did not provide for his store. What other types of electronic systems could have been used to reduce shrinkage?

6.

Inventory Control

I always found **stockroom employees**, whom I called "the guys," to be some of the most fun people to work with. They always had a way of turning **truck receiving**, or loading boxes all day, into one of the more fun and relaxed days at work. At least for part of a day, it was just us and a truck. No customers, no cashiers, just boxes and some laughs. Sometimes it was hot and stuffy, but we never seemed to mind.

Another one of my stockroom employees I loved working with was Mikey. Mikey was a teenager who always talked about his dreams of becoming a rapper. I don't know if it ever happened, as I've never listened to any rap record to know if he did, but for as young as he was he seemed very determined. He was a hard worker, and one our most reliable employees. He was always in a good mood, even when I found out later that his home life growing up wasn't easy on him. He was the kind of kid who would do anything you asked him to do, just as long as you asked him nicely.

Mikey and I always had a great relationship. Once he told me "Man, if anyone else ever asked me to come in on my day off I'd say No way. But you're cool, and you let me listen to music while I unload the truck.

Plus, I know you'll be out back slinging boxes with me." He wasn't wrong, at least about the music and boxes part. I never asked him to do anything I wouldn't do myself, and usually ended up doing it with him.

Technically I wasn't supposed to let him listen to music in the back of the store, and a few times I considered telling him that just to save myself from an afternoon of hip-hop. I really didn't want to listen to his music, and I knew he certainly didn't want to have me subject him to an afternoon of my favorite heavy metal albums. But, for Mikey, I always caved because I saw how hard he worked and how happy having his music made him.

"Look, if the district manager or anyone from corporate shows up, turn that off and if anyone asks I never let you listen to it. Otherwise, let's just get the boxes loaded and lunch is on me afterwards." Whenever we could, after receiving a truck, I'd order the two of us some fast food. We would spend our lunch break eating some French fries and laughing about our day lifting boxes. Mikey and I could always make each other laugh.

Receiving trucks always provided me with some stories I couldn't get working inside the store. One hot summer afternoon we smelled something bad. It didn't smell like a skunk or a rotten egg. That's not what this was. This was, bad. This seemed dead. We opened the back receiving door and found the stench was coming from the dumpster. Mikey quickly told me that since I got paid more it was my job to open the dumpster. I did, and found a garbage bag with what seemed to be some sort of dead body inside it. Again, I called the cops first and reported the scene.

"There's a dead body in the dumpster. It stinks really badly and it's been a few days since our dumpster was emptied. This could have been here a few days. Oh, and no we don't have a camera out back either."

The bad news is, it was a dead body inside a garbage bag. The good news was it wasn't human. It was a pig. I have no idea who decided throwing a dead pig in our dumpster made sense, but we were told that the police couldn't pick it up and we would have to wait until animal control came a few days later. Those days stunk.

When things didn't stink from rotting dead pigs, we were spending time trying to make sense of the **inventory control system** we had in place. At any job I have had before, **receiving inventory** was a tiring but simple process. The **manager on duty** (MOD) receives some sort of inventory report, and every box or item they receive gets verified on the list. If not done by **physical count**, the task could be completed much easier by simply scanning every item as you receive it. Our process was much simpler.

The company didn't have its own fleet of trucks or its own trucking organization. We would use various **commercial shipping companies** to distribute our **products** from one store to the next. I always imagined that within time we would eventually have our own trucking facility or at least enter in an agreement with one trucking company. In my time for the company, there was a regular rotation of different colored trucks with a revolving door of different truck drivers. The constant change in trucking companies became the second reason we kept a digital camera in the safe at all times.

Our trucks were packed in the corporate office. The 3 stores in our area were usually packed on one truck. Sometimes our truck also carried merchandise for other stores that were farther away. It was rare that any of our stores received enough merchandise to fill an entire trailer, so one truck usually carried inventory for at least 3 stores.

The trucks were always packed so that all the merchandise from one store was put in the truck, then some sort of barrier, usually simple cardboard, was placed between them so that we knew what was for each store. However, in the early days of the store we didn't have an electronic system of inventory receiving, despite the number of stores in the company growing, our inventory system stayed the same.

Once the truck was loaded and locked up, a small, usually orange zip tie was placed on the truck doors. Each of these zip ties had a unique number. The ties were used in such a way that I couldn't open the doors of the trailer without breaking the seal. The logic was that as long as the seal on the zip tie wasn't broken, the truck hadn't been tampered with, and all of the merchandise would be intact from when it left the distribution center. Receiving a truck simply meant taking a digital photo of the zip tie seal and sending it off to the corporate office. We didn't need to count boxes or verify against any sort of **itemized log**. We relied on the same digital cameras used for our visual audits.

We were told this photo would prove we received everything that was intended on the truck. When Mikey would start unloading that truck, he would unload every box until he reached the truck **divider** that had another store's number on it. He was happy he never had to scan boxes or write anything down. If he got the boxes off the truck quickly and loaded into our stockroom neatly, I was happy with Mikey and the company was happy with us. We trusted the company, as we had no reason not to.

One morning, Mikey and I were having an easy truck receiving day. The weather was nice, the truck showed up on time, and unloading the truck gave me an opportunity to let another manager manage the sales floor. He had a cd player loaded with an underground rapper he was looking to emulate, and the boxes were coming off the truck fast. We had developed an efficient system of stacking and sliding and carrying to save our backs whenever possible. I can only imagine every store for the company had developed their own ways of unloading, and this method worked for us.

That day, we were the first stop on that truck and our shipment wasn't very big. We could see the barrier to the next stores' inventory wasn't that far back so our job wouldn't be very difficult today. As we started getting closer to the barrier, we started noticing there were things written on the divider that was more than what we usually saw. We moved boxes out of the way and saw what was written.

"Help us! We are trapped against our will at the corporate office!"

Mikey and I looked at each other in a bit of shock. We weren't sure if we were supposed to laugh, or if we had just uncovered something. We didn't know if we were being pranked or if we had just discovered a ring of employees that needed saving. We grabbed our camera and started taking photos. I ran into the office and got on the phone with the corporate office.

"That's right. The divider says that there are people in the distribution center that are trapped and can't get out and they wanted our help. We need to call the police near the corporate office and save these people" I told the corporate employee over the phone. He immediately assumed I was joking, as there was no way this could have happened.

"Well, I took photos. I'm going to start uploading the photos and send them to you guys."

"No, don't send the photos, just ignore it entirely and receive the truck as usual" I was told.

My next conversation was with my district manager who seemed much less happy about it. I sent the photos to her and told her to make some phone calls and see what could have been done with them. I finished receiving our merchandise, pulled that cardboard barrier out of the truck and into our recycling bin. I affixed a new numbered zip tie onto the truck and uploaded the photo to show the truck was ready to be sent to the next destination.

After that, I started being a bit less thankful for the simplicity of our truck receiving. I became a lot less trustful that what was being put on the trucks was accurate. When I started being told we didn't have merchandise in our visual audits that we were supposed to have, I stopped blaming the visual department and started blaming the distribution center.

What if, all that time, we were supposed to have the new polo shirt? What if we actually were supposed to have those new boot-cut jeans on the table? What if there were boxes that were never put on the truck, and how were we supposed to know? More importantly, what if those truck loaders were really trapped there against their will at the corporate office. The zip ties and photographs never told us what happened to them. I think all of this explains why anytime I order something online I track the shipping constantly, sweating until the box shows up on my doorstep.

Chapter 6 Key Terms

1. Commercial shipping company
2. Divider
3. Inventory control system
4. Itemized log
5. Manager-on-duty
6. Physical count

7. Products
8. Receiving inventory
9. Stockroom employee
10. Truck receiving

Chapter Takeaways

- A proper system of inventory control and receiving merchandise is required for any company.
- For a company to survive, a proper inventory system needs to be established with focus placed on the trucking, as well as receiving processes.

Discussion Questions

1. How did the company verify each store received the proper merchandise? What ways could this have been done more efficiently?
2. Why did the author begin to lose trust in the company's inventory receiving? Do you agree with his distrust? Why or why not?
3. Mikey liked his job in the stockroom. What reasons did he like his job? Would you like this job? Explain your answers.
4. The author explained that he had a positive working relationship with Mikey. Why was this possible?

Time Off

In retail, **district managers** are the person that **store-level employees** always dreaded seeing. Cashiers know anytime that the district manager shows up that we are going to have to be on our best behavior. No more music in the stockroom, we would all have to have shirts tucked in, and we had to be sure to wear our uncomfortable ear pieces in our walkie-talkies. Everyone needed to do everything by the book. District managers were the one insight to corporate that many of the part-time employees would ever see, and none of my part-timers ever wanted to have to work on the day that they were doing a store visit.

Our district manager's name was Beverly. She was the manager who interviewed and hired me, so I always felt that if nothing else, my paycheck, my job and my health insurance had her to thank. While my salary was modest, I was glad to have a salary and I was making ends meet. I was also working for an exciting company. I kept hearing on the news that our company was one of the biggest success stories in recent history. I can remember being proud when I told my friends from home that my company was the one to keep their eyes on. I had Beverly to thank.

I'm not entirely sure that Beverly liked me very much, which I blame entirely on my rather rebellious nature. While I gave her no reason to necessarily dislike me, I have always struggled at interpersonal relationships. Another lesson my grandfather taught me was to "Never be a 'yes' man." He had always told me about those employees who suck up to their bosses, and rely on their ability to schmooze over their ability to work. His entire career had been based on outworking anyone he ever worked with. For the rest of my life, his message has stuck with me. I always felt Beverly favored the employees who sucked up more than I did. Likely, she just preferred employees who didn't always have a hundred complaints to throw at her when she would walk into the store.

Visits from Beverly weren't all bad and they often came with some perks. District managers travelled for a living, going from hotel to hotel and lived off a corporate credit card. I can remember being jealous of someone who got to eat out at every meal, thinking how great it must have been. The corporate meal policy simply limited meals to "casual dining," and when she visited our stores it usually meant taking one of the managers with her out to sports bar type restaurants. There is no meal tastier than a meal paid for with a corporate credit card, and she got them 3 times a day.

Beverly also spent a considerable amount of time in her car. She absolutely loved her black sedan, which was the first car I had ever ridden in that was equipped with an on-board GPS system. The first time I rode in her passenger seat I watched in amazement as she simply pushed a few buttons and found where the nearest steakhouse was located. Before I had a chance to tell her where to turn, her car was giving us turn-by-turn directions. This was the first time in my life I was ever given the option to order whatever I wanted off a restaurant menu. I just ordered a sandwich like everyone else, but otherwise, I'd have gotten a steak, and maybe even dessert. Beverly swiped her corporate card and paid for herself, as well as myself and 2 other managers from my store. We all left full and happy.

As soon as we returned to the store, it was all business. It was the beginning of **4th quarter**. For anyone in retail, the month of October was always a month of planning and preparation. Our store was always busy in the late spring and early summer. One June particularly we couldn't keep men's plaid shorts in stock. I had never owned a pair before, but when we started receiving bigger shipments of them to keep up with demand, I made sure to pick up a few pair. I had to admit they were rather comfortable and looked great with a pair of the new casual line of Starbury shoes.

We were much slower during 3rd **quarter**. Kids were back to school, and business wouldn't pick up again until things got a bit closer to Christmas. In a traditional retail calendar, our busy season was going to come in 4th quarter. October in retail feels like a calm before the storm or that overwhelming feeling of dread.

Beverly reminded us about our schedule for the months of November and December. As managers, we usually worked 5 days a week, and we were asked to work a minimum of 10-hour days. It seemed like a lot of time, but never seemed like enough time to get things done. However, during the holiday season we would be all working 6-day work weeks, and we would get extra **paid time off** after the New Year. I thought this sounded like a pretty good deal. A little **quid pro quo**. I didn't mind an extra day a week, especially when I'm busy, time tends to go by quickly. That extra time off in January would be well deserved.

I can remember wondering what that famous **nine to five job** I had heard so much about from my friends in other industries must have felt like. Weekends, late nights, early mornings, and sometimes overnights were all a part of my regular routine. When everyone else was enjoying their federal holidays, I was working. At first I would get upset at all of my friends who had the weekends off, but eventually it just became a part of my world. I made my own Friday night on a Tuesday. My cook-out would be a few days after the 4th, and I knew I'd be eating turkey a few days after Thanksgiving. Once I learned to embrace the fact that I did things on retail time, I stopped being upset and started just living it. Nurses and police officers could do it, and their jobs had to be harder than mine was. If they could do it, so could I.

Retail workers don't just work through holidays, they simply just work through everything. Appointments can always be rescheduled, and we can always get to the bank tomorrow. We also learn to work through being sick. Every retail manager has their own cold medicine cocktail. When I'd start feeling sick, I knew the routine. I'd take med-icine at bed time, less-drowsy medicine through the day. I'd consume vitamin c pills like candy, and drink orange juice by the gallon. There was no amount of feeling bad that could keep a good retail employee away from the store, especially when things were busy, and things were always busy.

The real problem though, was that I didn't really have any option but to go into work when I was sick. In a lot of jobs, people quickly learn that you aren't that important and their absence doesn't keep the office from opening. In retail, when someone has a set of keys to the store, sometimes if they're not there the store literally won't open. No one really has the option of not going in. So, I would suck it up, take my cold medicine, and go to work.

Every time I was sick I'd tell myself I'll actually be fine, and as I was still young, I knew I would. Sure, it might be a rough day, but I've done it before and I'll be able to do it again. I'd show up and tell my hourly employees I felt terrible and was going to do my best to work in the back all day so that I don't get everyone sick. Usually that means they would do their best to leave me alone, and sometimes it even means my sick day ends up being just a quieter day in the stockroom. It's not quite chicken soup and a movie, but it beats running around the store all day.

Except sometimes, I didn't just have a cold. One evening I had off from work, I had become violently ill. I couldn't keep anything down and spent the night throwing up like I hadn't since a night in college where I had spent a bit too much time with a bottle of bourbon. My face was every shade of purple, my skin was as white as a ghost. I couldn't keep water down, and was becoming quickly dehydrated. As the morning came, I knew there was no chance I'd ever be able to leave the bathroom let alone get into the office. I had been working full time since I was 16, and for the first time in my life I was about to call out sick. I tried to convince myself not to, but when I realized I barely had the energy to pick up my phone to dial the store, I knew I had to do it. I called Beverly, and was about to tell her that she'd have to get one of the other managers or someone from one of the other stores today.

"Sorry, I'd never do this, but I've been throwing up last night. I don't know if I have severe food poisoning or if it's a really bad stomach flu, but I need to get to a doctor and there's absolutely no way I can come in to the store today. I have **sick days** and **personal days** banked to use." I told her, likely sounding rather pathetic.

"Today isn't a good day for you to call out. I'll need you in the store right away." Beverly said.

"I literally can't stop throwing up. There's no way I can actually work today" I tried explaining.

"Like I said, today isn't a good day. Thanks"

Click.

Did my district manager just tell someone with a stomach flu they couldn't call out? The thought that I could quickly infect every other employee and customers in the store was the least of my concerns. My ability to even drive in to work seemed in question. I have absolutely no idea how I did it, but I did make it into work that morning. I spent the entire shift running in and out of the bathroom, but the store was opened and I did my job. The show must go on, right?

Ever since that day, I still find it hard to take a sick day, or even consider not showing up to work. It wasn't until years after leaving retail that I'd even consider staying home sick, or keeping my car parked in my driveway during a blizzard. Every time I'm sick, I still ask myself, "is today a good day to stay home?"

Chapter 7 Key Terms

1. 3rd quarter
2. 4th quarter
3. nine to fivejob
4. District manager
5. Paid time off
6. Personal days
7. Quid pro quo
8. Sick days
9. Store-level employees

Chapter Takeaways

- Retail employees tend to work a considerable amount of time during 4th quarter. Salaried employees are sometimes reimbursed with additional time off after the holidays.
- District managers often have a difficult relationship with store-level employees.
- Companies can spend a lot of money on district managers' food and travel.
- Working while sick can be a reality for retail employees. However, employees' health should be respected by their employer.

Discussion Questions

1. Why do store-level employees sometimes dislike when a district-manager comes into the store? Would you dislike when they arrive? Explain your answers.
2. What might a "typical" work schedule look like for a store manager? Would you enjoy this type of schedule? Why or why not?
3. The author was asked to work an extra day every week during the holiday season with the anticipation that he would be given extra paid-time-off in January. Does this seem fair? Why or why not?
4. The author describes a morning when he tried asking for the day off due to being sick but he was told he had to report to work anyway. How do you feel about this? Was this just his district manager trying to keep the business open? Explain your answers.

8.

Black Friday

Outside of my hometown in Pennsylvania was a large shopping mall that was shaped like a handgun. Its shape always led to conspiracy theories of influence from organized crime. The mall was always busy because shoppers from outside the state would arrive to enjoy not having to pay sales tax on clothing. The number of restaurants and retail outlets that opened a short distance from the mall seem to grow every year. It wasn't until years later that I realized the irony of leaving home to find a management job in retail a few states away.

I was in middle school when I first truly discovered Black Friday. Black Friday was the day after Thanksgiving when everything went on sale. In the digital age, much of the shopping we do is on our phones from the comfort of our own living rooms, but Black Friday used to be a national sport. It was my favorite sport to participate in. At my hometown mall it was always a spectacle. I always felt they should sell concessions just for viewers. I made it a point to go out on Black Friday just to watch frenzied shoppers trying to get their hands on the biggest sale item, whether it be a new video game, toy, or a big discount on bath towels. Black Friday was like the big game for me, and has been my favorite holiday ever since.

Working at Steve and Barry's we knew that our entire calendar revolved around the holiday season and that Black Friday was the beginning of everything. The other stores in our shopping center would be gearing up weeks in advance. On November 1st, our surrounding stores would somehow have all the Halloween costumes and candy off the floor and their stores would seem like you were at the North Pole before you knew it. Black Friday was not only a big day for retailers, but a highly competitive one. Every retailer knew that the key to surviving was through sales during Christmas, and Black Friday was your one shot to start it all. It seemed like a big game, but to retail companies, it was a game of life and death.

Our company had so quickly become a major player in the retail world, that we had huge expectations to be one of the top stores for Christmas of 2006. We had also learned that only so much of the retail world can be planned out well in advance. We knew that Christmas was on December 25th, and that Thanksgiving would fall on the fourth Thursday in November. Other than that, so much of what was going to happen for Christmas would happen just-in-time. We could **push the market** only so much, and a lot would end up being reactionary. It's the same reason why many of the **big box retailers** are hesitant to release their Black Friday sales too early. It can result in a **price war** to gain as much of the **market share** as possible.

On the week before the big day, we started working on **assigning shifts** on the employee schedule. As a manager I knew I'd be there, and I knew to be careful to have all my best employees scheduled with me. We would have to schedule the guys in receiving for extra hours the days before to get boxes loaded and schedule extra employees to get merchandise staged in the backroom. I can remember renting a history documentary and feeling like I was a war planner trying to stage the invasion of Normandy on D-Day. I had my best troops scheduled, and all our best products ready to sell to the frenzy of customers coming in for the **door busters**.

The just-in-time philosophy was a part of our day-to-day lives at Steve and Barry's, but I never took it as poor planning. I always figured we were a young company that was paving the way for bigger things, and there would be no way that we could plan for everything. Just like that call we got about rearranging the store for Stephon, getting a package delivered would sometimes be filled with **ceiling-hung signs, endcaps, free standing display units,** or other types of **point-of-sale signage.** They would often be full of the new promotions we were running, or full-size window decorations to attract customers. It wasn't uncommon to get these packages the day before, or even the day of, a big sale. When we hadn't yet received any signage for Black Friday, we weren't alarmed. This was just how the crazy world of retail worked when your company was young and exciting.

Wednesday, two days before Black Friday, we had not yet received any communication regarding the details of our big sales that were coming. We didn't receive any new signs, but we knew that we had plenty of signage in the storage room to accommodate anything the company would throw at us. At this point, I had started wondering what the game plan would be. I assumed the company was waiting until the last minute to let us know what we were doing. With our prices being low already, and with the pressure on our company to succeed, I knew the sales were going to be huge. Would the whole store be on sale? Would we be giving things away?

Friday morning came and I arrived at 6 a.m. with the largest sized coffee I could find. I had most of my store employees scheduled to work that morning, and we were ready to have the biggest day in the company's history. We had a store meeting before opening and I gave my best pep talk. In our company we were encouraged to have **start-of-shift huddles,** and I tried to act like a good coach when firing my employees up for the big day. We were going to win and win big.

Unsurprisingly, there were a large number of customers waiting outside for our store opening at 8 a.m. In our store we always opened the store 5 minutes before our posted opening time, which was in place to allow our mall stores to have customers in our stores before any other. I unlocked the front doors and a few dozen customers came in looking to clean out our store. It was already relatively late in the morning, as many stores started their sales as early as 4:00, but we were certainly still within the window of opportunity. We weren't going to be the first place customers went for their Christmas shopping, but the line outside showed us that we were going to be one of the places they went with cash in hand. This seemed like it would prove to be a great start to the season.

We opened the doors, and people rushed in. Many of them had bags from the neighboring stores, and I watched some of the groups coming into the store split up in a determined fashion.

"You hit up the Starbury section, I'll head to Bitten and then we can meet up at the cash registers. We don't want anything sold out" were among the methods I heard families and friends discuss with each other. They were seasoned Black Friday shoppers and they had a plan. Some of them even brought their own walkie-talkies to communicate with each other across stores. Watching them shop was incredible.

After a quick lap around the store, an early customer came up to the cash register and in a confused tone asked me a very blunt question.

"So, where are the sales?"

That was a good question. My employees and I had spoken before opening about the company's plans for the day. I had to tell them that we had not received any word about sales and that the last thing I had heard was the company's position was that due to our already low prices, there was no need for a sale. So, I did my best to explain to the customer.

"Well, here at Steve and Barry's we have some of the lowest prices in town. Everything in the Starbury line is $14.98 or less, and even Sarah Jessica Parker's clothing are all $19.98 or under. You'll find great deals here!"

"Yeah, that's how the prices here always are. I mean, what about the actual sales. It's Black Friday." She quickly explained, and just as quickly, left with an empty bag. Over the course of the next hours we saw customers leave our store as empty handed as they had entered, with a bit of a surprised look on their faces. We quickly saw for ourselves that Black Friday shoppers are out for sales.

By early afternoon, we received a call from someone at corporate telling us that we needed to quickly put up some signs and get a big sale throughout the entire store. The problem was it was too late. My store full of employees had spent the morning doing next to no business, as we looked out the front windows and saw all the commotion at the nearby Target. We had missed Black Friday morning, and at this point, there was no getting it back.

I was never sure if it simply hadn't occurred to anyone in the company that sales on Black Friday were important, or if it was hubris in our price point. I had to imagine by the time we had received that phone call, our stores across the country had as hard of a morning as we did. I hoped not.

I still make it a point to visit as many retail stores as I can on Black Friday, and I still love watching all the commotion. I often find myself at big-box retail stores even when I have no intention on buying more than a cup of coffee in a drive thru. I often speak to news outlets about my thoughts on the big sales every year. I still remind them that just like those customers that left my store empty handed, I won't buy anything on my favorite holiday if it's not at least 40% off regular price.

Chapter 8 Key Terms

1. Assigning shifts
2. Big-box retailer
3. Black Friday
4. Ceiling-hung signs
5. Door buster
6. End caps
7. Free-standing display units
8. Market share
9. Point-of-purchase signage
10. Price war
11. Pushing a market
12. Start-of-shift huddle

Chapter Takeaways

- Black Friday begins the busiest time of the year and much of a retailer's success hinges upon a successful start of the holiday season.
- Steve and Barry's missed the opportunity to capitalize on early holiday shoppers.
- Too much faith was put in the regularly low prices that the behavior of holiday bargain shoppers was ignored.

Discussion Questions

1. Why is Black Friday so important to retailers?
2. What are some ways that store managers can prepare for holiday shoppers?
3. Why were customers leaving Steve and Barry's empty handed? Do you think the pricing strategy the company used was correct?
4. The author tried to defend the lack of sales to a customer, but was unsuccessful. What could the company have done to be more successful on Black Friday?

9.

Christmas Party

It's hard not to get at least a little excited every year once the holiday season is in full swing. Christmas has its own sights, smells, and sounds. Everything is decorated in red and green; Santa is everywhere and no matter how hard we try we can't escape hearing Jingle Bells. Some of us grab our ugly sweaters, some of us hang a mistletoe and hope for the best. We watch our favorite Christmas movies, which in my case includes any action movie that takes place on December 25th.

While many people across the globe acknowledge the religious significance of the holiday season, whether it be a celebration of Christmas, Kwanzaa or Chanukah, the common denominator of the holiday season is it's supposed to be a season of joy. It might be the only time of the year that we see some of our loved ones, or the time of year that we finally remember to show our love for those around us. Growing up in Pennsylvania, I was not one to dream of a white Christmas, but I'd certainly look forward to a season of joy. In recent years I've become a fan of making homemade fudge, to the joy (or dismay) of my colleagues and friends. I spend the month of December fattening up everyone I know.

Many of us have visions in our minds of a cold winter morning where Santa left us our favorite toy under the tree. We all remember there being that one present we spent our childhood dreaming about. For me it was usually a video game, or an action figure to add to my collection. The truly life altering joy of finally opening the present, or the horror of finding out you were the only kid on the block who didn't get one for Christmas, is an image that will be forever burned into our psyche. As kids we wrote our lists, and worked extra hard to keep our grades up so we would get that special gift. I didn't always get what I wanted for Christmas, but it still always seemed like a special morning. As adults, we see just how long Santa's helpers have to wait in line at the stores to get those highly sought after gifts every year. The season of joy always seems to end up being the season of shopping and depleted bank accounts.

In retail, I'd get a front row seat against the boards to see the stress the average parent goes through to find the gifts their kids want, and I could see how hard it is for many of them to pay for all the things they want to buy. Black Friday is chaotic, but customers are excited and mostly happy. Every once in a while a fight might break out between two customers over a newly released video game, but it's rare anyone gets hurt. The problem is, that's only the excitement of Black Friday. Shortly after, the fun wears off and the fear of the holiday coming starts to sink in. Every day until Christmas is harder than the day before. The stress starts to rise, the general attitude of customers starts to deteriorate, and the amount of theft and shoplifting you'll see grows by the hour.

I saw all kinds of schemes. Customers will often try anything if it means getting the things they want that they can't afford. On Christmas Eve of 2006, I was paged to the cash registers to speak to a clearly belligerent customer. She had explained her situation to one of my cashiers first, but the overwhelmed and frightened cashier knew she would need a manager to help her. I came to the front of the store, and the conversation went something like this.

"Happy Holidays, I'm the store manager here at Steve and Barry's. My cashier said you were having a problem, what can I do to help?" I did my best to put on my biggest Christmas smile.

"I came in yesterday and bought a bunch of clothes and when I got home, I realized your cashier never gave me all of my bags. I paid for things and never got them. I need you to give me what I paid for." She looked very serious and was already yelling.

She continued to tell me what the employee looked like who was working yesterday. Not only did her description not describe any employee that was working at that time, it was a rather generic enough description that it seemed almost funny. I also knew that had any bags been accidentally not given to a customer they'd have been left behind the counter with a note attached. Usually in management you learn that, if something smells fishy, it probably is.

As any retail manager would do, though, I very quickly apologized. She then told me what she wanted me to do about it. Since we kept a few bags of things that she had purchased the night before, she would just go through the store and grab the merchandise that she should have been sent home with, and I could just bag them and let her have them today. In all the hustle and bustle of the holidays, it would have been easy for any of us to fall for that one. Luckily, I told her that simply wasn't possible.

"Here's the number for the corporate office. You can give them a call. While I feel awful for what happened, I'm not authorized to give you any merchandise without you paying for it today. I bet if you give them a call then can help you get things sorted" I lied. When in doubt, always have the customer call corporate, and always be sure to call corporate before the customer does so you can give them a heads up.

The customer quickly became furious and told me that I needed to give her all the items in my store that she wanted. I continued to tell her to call the corporate office and talk to them. She eventually told me she was friends with the Governor, as well as local news anchors, and that I would be sorry if I didn't give her what she wanted. After screaming at me and causing a big scene, she eventually left. She never did call the corporate office and I never heard from the Governor.

One of my cashiers came up to me afterward and told me she felt awful for me having to deal with that customer, and that she had never seen me so frustrated before. I told her it was ok, I thanked her for her concern, and said I was just happy it was me she was yelling at instead of her. It might have ruined my Christmas Eve, but as long as it didn't ruin any of my employees', everything was ok in my book.

Throughout the Christmas season I had done everything I could to try to improve **employee morale**. I knew they were spending their nights and weekends in our busy store instead of spending it with their families. I knew we'd be asking them to show up a little earlier, work a little later, and be a whole lot busier than they were used to. Normally an employee would be terminated only in the case of a **no-call no-show**, but during the holidays they could be fired for simply **calling-off** or not being **punctual**. We weren't going to pay **time and a half** or give them any sort of **holiday bonus**, but I could at least do everything I could to make them feel appreciated. I at least wanted them to know we were in this thing together.

"So, are we going to have a big store Christmas Party?" I was asked by Megan, one of our cashiers who had worked for the store longer than I had. She told me the previous year they closed early on a weekday and had a nice Christmas party, and she said how it really made her love working here.

"Sorry, I'd really love to have one but I just got off a **conference call** with the corporate office and they told us we were not to have any official holiday parties. We could have one off site after the holidays if we wanted, but it had to be outside of normal **business hours** and the company wasn't going to pay for it." She looked a bit disappointed, but I assured her that money was tight in the company and that we were trying to really be successful this year and that it was for the good of the whole company that we didn't spend any money on things like parties this year.

A few days after Christmas we received our **company newsletter** in the mail which was addressed to employees. The front page of the newsletter was usually filled with anecdotes from the corporate office, letters from various vice presidents, or getting to know you columns about a new director that was hired. We would sometimes have a good laugh at the titles of some employees that were hired, such as one whose job we jokingly called the "director of corporate fun." She would call our stores from time to time to tell us how exciting things were. I also remember sharing with my store every time we would make the top 10 in sales across the whole company.

While the previous month's newsletter had contained pictures from a movie that was a favorite of both mine and one of the company's executives, Nathan, this particular newsletter was a bit out of the ordinary. The front page of the newsletter was filled with photos of the corporate office's Christmas party. The party was held in a large formal room in Manhattan and the party seemed to be rather elaborate. The newsletter referenced how the company paid for the party to honor the corporate office employees' hard work and dedication. The newsletter almost seemed to be bragging about how great of a party they were given.

I was mad, and I quickly threw the newsletter in the trash. I knew if any of my employees saw it, I'd have to try to justify a lavish corporate Christmas party after telling them they couldn't have even a small get together. There was absolutely no way I was going to share that piece of information with anyone that I worked with. I knew I'd never be able to convince them of what I couldn't even convince myself. Our **turnover** was already high enough, and we couldn't afford to lose more employees.

When I attend an office holiday party now, it usually takes me a couple of free martinis and a plateful of hors d'oeuvres before I can drown my guilt. I wonder how much all those cocktails cost, and what the fancy country club downtown charges my employer. I can't help but feel a little guilty about it. I can't help but think of what else we could be doing with the money we are spending. I also can't help but want to find Megan and invite her for a long overdue Christmas celebration. Maybe then I can feel like I don't need to fill my own stockings with coal.

I've never in my entire life received a Christmas bonus, but I seem to always talk to people who get them every year. In retail, I never got a bonus either but for those of us that were salaried managers, we did receive a Christmas present in the mail. A few days before Christmas, I had a package addressed to me from Long Island, NY. I opened the package and saw a note that said "For all your hard work, from Steve and Barry's." I quickly opened the package, to find an oversized, 5-pound chocolate bar inside. I was a bit dumbfounded, and wasn't sure why anyone would pay to ship 5 pounds chocolate, nor could I understand why anyone would give someone that as a present. At least I couldn't say they didn't send me something. Maybe the next year I'd get one of those fancy watches everyone always talks about.

Chapter 9 Key Terms

1. Business hours
2. Calling-off
3. Company newsletter
4. Conference call
5. Employee morale
6. Employee turnover
7. Holiday bonus
8. No-call no-show
9. Punctuality
10. Time and a half

Chapter Takeaways

- The holiday season can bring out the worst in customers and make it especially frustrating and stressful for store-level employees.
- Expectations for hourly employees can be high, especially during the holiday season. They should be treated fairly and rewarded for their efforts.
- A company shouldn't provide home-office employees with rewards that a company is unwilling to provide the rest of the company. It could lessen employee morale more than other factors.

Discussion Questions

1. What was the scheme a customer tried to use to obtain free merchandise? How would you have handled it?

2. What are some of the expectations of hourly employees during the holiday season? Do you think these expectations are fair? Why or why not?
3. Why would the holiday season be especially hard to keep a positive employee morale?
4. The author referenced being offended by the party showcased in the newsletter and didn't show it to other employees. How would you have felt if you saw this newsletter? Would you have shared it with the rest of the staff? Why or why not?

My Flight to Corporate

Working in a store that sold a large amount of **licensed apparel** from a number of colleges often made me feel like a bit of a fraud. I admittedly know very little about college sports. I've never even seen a college basketball game, and I don't bet on the tournament pools either. Before working there, I couldn't have named more than a handful of collegiate team names. I didn't know that certain shades of colors could represent rival sports teams. One time, a fellow manager told me she went to a large southern college. I ignorantly followed that up by "Oh? Where's that?" I still don't know where that school is located and I'm not sure she ever forgave me for it.

On April 16, 2007, at the campus shooting in Blacksburg, Virginia, 32 people were killed and 17 others were wounded in what was, at the time, the deadliest mass shooting by a lone gunman in the United States history. I had only heard briefly about a campus incident on the radio on my commute to work, but didn't know the extent of the situation. I blocked it out while I worked, but I heard the heartbreaking news later in the day. Like everyone else, I didn't know what to do, or what to say.

By early that afternoon, our store had flooded with customers coming in to buy shirts, hats, and hoodies to show their school support. Until that day, I had never heard of their sports team, but now it's a name I will certainly never forget. Within a few hours we sold completely out of everything we stocked with their logo on it. I never knew how much a college logo on a sweatshirt could mean to someone before that day. I had also never seen that much solidarity among customers.

As spring was arriving, and the retail world would stay a bit slower until summer came, I started thinking about what my future would hold and whether or not it would be with this company. I was still young, and having survived a big 4th quarter, I found myself not tired, but energized. I began thinking it was time to start making my imprint on the company and move up, or it was time to walk out the front door. With all the growth in our company, I didn't want out, I wanted in and I wanted up. I saw myself moving to New York, and was waiting to pounce on any opportunity I was given.

One morning, I logged into the SOC to check my daily communications, I saw an email addressed to store managers with an invitation for us to apply for a new position of a **training director** for the company. The **job description** read that this would be a position in the corporate office that would oversee all of the training of managers and corporate employees. If any of us were interested, we simply needed to send them a message and let them know. I felt I was qualified and in the back of my mind had always considered a career in teaching. I sent my notification immediately.

Up until this point, the only **job promotion** opportunity that any store employee had been offered was to become part of the **store opening team**. While I originally saw myself as part of that team, one of the guys who trained with me in Long Island, a former car salesman like myself, had taken one of the positions and told me how hard it was. I knew quickly it wasn't for me. Anytime I talked to him in person, he seemed to regret the decision to leave a store and start travelling with the store openers. His job was important but it seemed especially hard on him and far from glamourous.

The store openers would oversee getting new stores opened and operating. They were given a corporate credit card and flown out to a site of a new store. The store could be anywhere in the country. It might be partially ready, or it might not have been started. It might be an empty building, or in the case of one of the stores I managed, it might have been in a building that had been unused for so long it became a makeshift homeless shelter. They often worked all day, 7 days a week, and the turnover rate was ridiculously high. I'm glad I never accepted that position, but this newly announced training director seemed like a perfect fit.

A week or two went by, and I was usually so busy running my store that I had almost completely forgotten I even applied for the position. It reminded me of how I had forgotten originally applying to work for the company. I had very little expectation of getting the job, since I assumed every store manager for the company was going to apply. I'd later find out I was the only one who did. Then the phone rang, and it was someone asking to speak to me in the office.

"Hi, are you the store manager? Are you in the office alone? Can you close the door?" a very nice woman with a Long Island accent asked me. I didn't know what this phone call was going to be about, but I took it rather seriously. I closed the door, and sat down at my desk.

"We received your application to work at the corporate office. Are you still interested?"

"Why yes, I am, and I'm so glad you called. I've been hoping to talk to someone about the opportunity." I said, trying to hide my nerves. I felt this was my opportunity to change my life. This was the phone call that was about to give me my shot, and nothing was going to stand between myself and a new career as a training director. I had to get this right.

"When is your next day off?" she asked.

"Coincidentally, I'm off tomorrow." I replied.

"We will need you to fly up to the corporate office tomorrow. The thing is, we need for you to not tell anyone you're coming. Don't tell anyone in your store, don't tell your district manager, or anyone else who works for the company. So, make sure you have tomorrow off and we will call you shortly with your flight details."

My excitement rose instantly. For the first time, instead of feeling out of the loop, I felt I was being trusted with company secrets.

I couldn't figure out why being flown in to the corporate office would be so secretive. Maybe they just don't want to spark resentment from other employees? Or maybe, this is a test. I convinced myself they must be testing me to see if I'm capable of holding company secrets and doing exactly as I'm told. I followed their instructions to the letter. No other employee in or out of my store would know of my secret mission to fly to Long Island and interview to be the next director of training.

After landing, I walked off the plane and saw a driver holding a sign that just said "Steve and Barry's." I knew that was my ride into the office. The driver nicely greeted me and said he looked forward to escorting me to Port Washington. When we pulled up outside the office, he handed me the card to sign. I must have been feeling rather important that day, because I signed off on a big tip just like I felt the new corporate director of training should do.

When I walked in the front door of the home office, I said my name and that I was here to interview with one of the vice presidents, Nathan. Knowing we had similar taste in movies, I was confident this had to go well. He looked much younger than I had pictured a company exec-utive, feeling he could have been younger than I was. I had been to the office before, but that was during a guided tour during training. While most of the employees I had met were younger, I had never seen it during normal business hours, and I watched as people moved fran-tically across the room. Tensions were obviously high and there was a strong sense of urgency sprinkled with chaos. I got the sense that every day might be just as chaotic.

Nathan greeted me and said "Things aren't normally this crazy. Everyone here is upset because we changed caterers here and no one likes the food the company gives. We all liked the food we were given before. Hopefully they'll get over it soon enough."

I didn't know how to take that. At first, I thought he was joking, but as I walked down the hall I heard some grumbling about catering. Before we stopped off at his office, he asked me if I wanted a cup of coffee.

"Thanks, but I'm not much of a coffee drinker." I lied. Coffee sounded great, but I wasn't sure if I was supposed to accept or not.

I chose to turn it down, assuming I'd be able to give the impression of someone who doesn't need a cup of coffee to handle his job.

"Oh, but you have to see this thing." He showed me a display of coffee pods and a style of coffee maker I had never before seen. "You can have whatever kind of coffee you want, and this just makes it for you one cup at a time. We love this thing around here." I told him I'd gladly take a cup, and I pointed at whichever one seemed the most exciting. He popped in the Irish Cream coffee pod I quickly got a piping hot custom cup of coffee.

When we got to his office, he told me to sit down and immediately hit me with the hardest interview question I've ever been asked in my life.

"So, please explain to me why you were asked to fly up to corporate and yet you didn't even tell your district manager. I called her before you got here and she said she never knew you were coming. Did you really think you'd have a chance of getting this job if your district manager didn't even refer you? She's supposed to be your biggest advocate."

I must have turned six shade of purple. Or maybe, I turned ghostly white. I could feel a bead of sweat dripping from my forehead.

"I didn't tell her because the recruiter who called me told me I wasn't allowed to tell anyone and specifically said not to tell my district manager. I wanted you to know that I can keep a secret when I'm asked to." I tried to explain.

"You actually listened to that? Well, that was your first mistake. Either way, we already hired someone for the job so I guess it doesn't matter."

Now my shock turned to a complete state of confusion. I flew up here to interview for a job that was already filled? I didn't know what to think. I didn't know what to say, and I suddenly felt really uncomfortable sitting in that chair. I asked then why I was there.

"Well, we thought it was pretty interesting that a store employee would think they could work at the corporate office so I figured I'd ask you some questions. What can you tell me from working in a store that we might like to know?"

I told him all about how I had an MBA and how I had quite a lot of advice about how to improve the company. I told him my thoughts about loss prevention, about store morale, and spent the most time talking to him about store training and communication. I explained how they could improve their **corporate communications** and increase **profitability**. I soon realized that I had a running list of these recommendations in my head. He quickly stopped me.

"Haha, ok. Well, I'd like you to meet Cameron, the head of another one of our departments. You can talk to him about seeing if he might want you to work with him, but just so you know, it wouldn't be any sort of promotion to what you're doing now. You'd still be in a store, you'd just be working directly for him and doing work for his department."

I had seen Cameron's name on the SOC before, but never knew who he was. I would come to find out he oversaw some of the company's operations. Cameron also looked younger than I was. I felt he had to have been immediately out of college. I was also surprised when, instead of asking me about the company, he asked me what my interests outside of work were. I told him how I used to be a touring musician and how much I liked listening to music.

He told me how much he loved pop music. It was the first time in my life a guy in his 20s had ever told me they liked boy bands. He continued, "Well, yeah I push out a lot of those notifications on the SOC (I quickly noticed he pronounced it "sock") and maybe we can talk about having you be one of the people in the store who works for me." He left the room and I never saw him again.

Shortly after, a secretary told me my day is done and to follow a younger woman out to the lobby and I can hang out there until my ride to the airport shows up. I'm not sure if I felt defeated or just plain confused. On my way down the hallway, I was stopped and hit with another surprise. "Oh, Steve wants to talk to you. He's down the hall in that **board room**."

I probably should have realized what she meant when she said Steve, it's clear I wasn't thinking correctly or paying attention to the fact that I was in the corporate office. I walked into a board room and saw 3 guys I had never seen before sitting beside Steve Shore, one of the owners of the company. Steve shakes my hand and asks why I think

I would be a good addition to the company. I wasn't sure if he knew I already worked there.

"Sir, I'm not even sure I know what job you're asking me about at this point." I said. It was probably not the best answer, but I was so beside myself at that point that it was all that I could muster. He shook my hand again, thanked me, and left the room.

On my flight back I was filled with emotions. I don't like flying, but I doubt I even noticed turbulence on that flight. I was embarrassed and felt ridiculed. I was mad that I felt I had been lied to. I was scared to go back to my store the next day and have an uncomfortable conversation with Beverly, my district manager who I already felt didn't like me very much. I was sad I would be going back to work in the same store I was working in the day before. I was disappointed I wouldn't be working for corporate. I was also, just a little bit thankful that I felt I had just dodged a huge bullet. If I wasn't so mentally exhausted, I would have gone out and bought a lottery ticket.

That was the last day I ever wished to work at the corporate office. That was the first day I began to question whether I should consider having any sort of future with the company. It was also the first time I wondered if the company itself would have a future at all.

Chapter 10 Key Terms

1. Board room
2. Corporate communications
3. Company executive
4. Job description
5. Job promotion
6. Licensed apparel
7. Profitability
8. Store opening team
9. Training director

Chapter Takeaways

- The company employed a number of young executives.
- The author was flown for an interview, but the job had already been filled.
- The author felt disrespected by the company, by the corporate employees, and lost motivation to continue working for the company.

Discussion Questions

1. The author mentions that the corporate office employees he met both seemed to be very young. Why do you think the author noticed this? Do you believe younger executives would have a positive or negative impact on the company? Explain your answers.
2. Why didn't the author tell anyone he was flying for the interview? What would you have done?
3. The author found out that the job he was applying for was already filled. Why do you think the company still sent him for an interview?
4. After this experience, the author begins to question his future with the company and the future of the company itself. What are some reasons for this? What would your opinion of the company have been had this been you?

11.

Hiring and Promotions

The big store I was managing had been over the 200ᵗʰ location for the company, and to outsiders it seemed like there was no end to our company's growth. We were hearing about new store openings all the time and always knew there would be another mall somewhere in the United States that needed a pick-me-up that our store could provide.

Nearby was a store that was located in a shopping mall that seemed to have been stuck somewhere in the 1970s. The mall had few stores, and even fewer customers. The location seemed like it would be better suited for a zombie movie than it would be as a location for a clothing store. When I first visited the store, I can remember how large the store was, and how simply dead feeling everything was inside.

In my training at the corporate office, I had been taught that much of the success of the company, as well as a lot of the growth, was due to a rather unique approach to retail locations. Our company would often open in malls that were losing business, or losing businesses. Our company had a knack for working out deals with malls that allowed our company to move into a mall for a fraction of the cost of a typical **retail lease**. The growing popularity of Steve and Barry's was seen as a way for those malls to drive businesses, and there was always hope for a snowball effect to happen that would spark businesses to open.

Despite the rapid growth within the company, the nearby store closure came as no surprise to any of us. I was never privy to the exact details of the lease that they had acquired in the mall, but the location was losing the company money. When that store closed, I wasn't sure if this was a sign that our company was being prudent about not keeping losing stores open, or if it was a sign that there might be rough times for our stores in the future.

As a store manager, I had begun to develop doubts that our company was being steered in the right direction. Part of my concern came from learning more about the history of the company and how the growth of our company had happened. The ability to acquire low-cost leases and save dying malls was only part of the equation.

We had always been told that the company originally started by Steve and Barry's, a secretary and a fax machine. The rest of the corporate employees came as they were needed. Many of them were hired as recruiters and many of the recruiters were then promoted into other positions within the company. The more I inquired about much of our corporate office, the more I had discovered that many of the directors and executives that were steering the company were new not only to retail, but new to the departments they were steering. This explained why Cameron, Nathan, and most of the employees I saw at the corporate office seemed younger than me. Most of them were.

Many of the corporate employees were hired at the office, and promoted to powerful positions within the company. While there is a lot to be said for **promoting from within**, there always seemed to be an air of inexperience as well as confusion any time we would speak with, or be given direction from, whichever corporate director we would be hearing from. My confidence level in anyone other than Steve or Barry themselves was at an all-time low.

At the store level, we did our absolute best to promote from within. Once we hired someone in the store, we made it clear to new employees that there were opportunities for them to be promoted. Employees could become **head cashiers**, and like Anne who handled the armed robber so well, they could become **keyholders**. A keyholder was a position that was paid hourly, but someone who was given the opportunity to take on a managerial role during their shifts. They could open and close the store, had access to the safe and manager's computer, and were given a large amount of latitude within the store. The position of keyholder was paid more than any other hourly employee, which made it an attractive position for anyone who didn't want to commit to the level that salaried management had.

One of the biggest reasons that we tried promoting from within was it was one of the few incentives we could give our hourly employees to work hard in our stores. The hourly employees never made much more than **minimum wage**, they weren't offered any sort of healthcare or any benefits, received absolutely no paid time off, and weren't even given any access to **direct deposit** for their paychecks. This meant that anytime there was a delay in our deliveries, our hourly employees would be receiving their checks late. Some of them rode the bus to work, and would have to wait for a bus ride home without a paycheck in their hands. At least the store managers knew our pay would be sitting comfortably in our bank accounts on payday.

Another problem that we had was due to the large number of young and inexperienced applicants that we would have applying to work in our stores. Any time we would need to hire hourly employees and it required **external candidates**, it was always a huge burden to dig through the piles of handwritten employment applications that we would have laying in a drawer by the cash registers. Many of the applications contained the same sort of information. They were mostly currently in high school, few of them had any previous jobs outside of being camp counselors or baby sitters, and many of them used their local pastor or football coach as the only **job references** they could list on the forms.

I developed my own method of digging through the applications to find the best employees. If I had a stack of 100 applications, my goal was to get that stack down to a manageable number of maybe 8 or 10. I would start by pushing any applications to the side that had quickly observable reasons to push them aside. Any application written in any color other than blue or black, any application with words crossed out or poor handwriting, any application with misspelled words, or any application that listed an email addresses with innuendos was imme-diately discredited.

This was the only way to try to find the young people who at least seemed to present themselves as more professional. Once I had this smaller list, I would find any applicants that had evening and week-end availability, and start calling them to offer them a chance to come in for an interview. My job was often made easier when I would hear what I felt was a stupid voicemail message. One time I called some-one whose voicemail was someone pretending to answer the phone but couldn't hear you. That was someone I never left a message for and never called back.

Once we had enough applicants to schedule interviews, I still had to figure out how to find out who might be the best people to hire. I would never offer a job to anyone who showed up to the interview late, but it was one simple question that I would ask each applicant that would serve as the best way for me to find employees that would end up being someone who might be promoted to a key carrier within time.

"Why do you want to work for Steve and Barry's" was always my first question I would ask during the interview. The question was easy, and I would accept any answer that the person would give providing they answered in a way that made me know they wanted to work for us, not that they were simply looking for a job. "I just need a job" or "I've never heard of your store but it looked nice from the outside" were the types of common answers that would make my job of crossing names off the list even easier.

The people I hired were the applicants who would tell me what made them choose us. These applicants clearly expressed that they wanted to work for Steve and Barry's, not just they wanted to work someone. Maybe it was they liked shopping here, they liked Starbury clothing line, or they were interested in fashion. I was just looking for any answer that gave me a clue that they had interest in our store, and had done some sort of preparation before walking into the interview.

While my crude method of interviewing wasn't magical and didn't always work, it seemed to be the best way that I could find for **employee screening** and hire the best that we could. However, one day I received a message from the corporate office explaining a new tool we had to use to hire employees. Anytime a new process or new tool was communicated to us in the SOC, I would tend to be a bit worried.

A new job application website was becoming a highly useful tool for unskilled job applicants and was widely used in the retail and service industry to find entry-level applicants. It worked like the other famous websites where a potential applicant could find job openings and apply for them. The difference was that this service only listed hourly jobs. It was a powerful tool for young people and unskilled workers to find hourly and entry-level jobs. We were told to expect to start seeing more of our applications come from there. I was immediately excited that we would have a tool that seemed much better than the old pen and paper applications.

The problem we saw was the directive that we were told specifically to always hire applicants from there first, before we looked at any in-store applications. If we needed applicants, we had to give priority to anyone who applied on through this service. If we had enough job openings, we were to hire everyone who applied through that website. I was never told about any sort of partnership that our company had with this website, but I was immediately concerned about losing the ability to screen applicants to work in my store, and the prospect of having to hire anyone without any additional level of in-store screening.

I'm not sure if my method of job screening was ever the best, but I can think of a long list of employees that worked for me in any of the stores I managed for the company that were fantastic employees. I lost many of them to other local companies who paid better or had better hours, and lost plenty when they graduated and went off to college. I might not have been able to keep them all, but at least I was able to do my best to find the best employees I could, and we did everything we could to make them feel like at least the managers in the store cared about them.

Chapter 11 Key Terms

1. Direct deposit
2. External candidates

3. Head cashier
4. Job reference
5. Keyholder
6. Minimum wage
7. Promoting from within
8. Retail lease

Chapter Takeaways

- A tactic used by the company was to place stores in less-than-ideal shopping centers and malls to receive a premium on their lease.
- The company lacked many incentives for hourly-employees but did use promotions to positions such as keyholder and head cashier to retain good employees.
- In-store managers used their own methods of screening applicants until the company pushed using a job application service for hourly employees.

Discussion Questions

1. What reasons would the owners of malls and shopping centers want to give Steve and Barry's a lower priced lease? How did this also benefit the company?
2. The author used promotions to retain strong employees. Why was this successful? Would you have wanted one of these positions? Explain your answers.
3. What ways did the author interview and screen applicants? Do you think this method was fair? Explain your answers.
4. The author was nervous and frustrated about using the new internet application service. Why do you think he felt this way? Do you agree this was a good direction for the company? Why or why not?

A Facelift

In October of 2007, I was starting to prepare, both mentally and physically, for my second holiday season with the company. The new store I was working at was considerably larger than the store that I spent my first holiday season, and I couldn't even imagine the **revenue** we would receive that year. Our store was not only one of the busiest, but also one of the physically largest stores in the company. Just walking from one end of the store to the other gave me a cramp in my legs.

The company's **position** in the market was changing. The company had officially dropped the words University Sportswear, becoming simply Steve and Barry's. As the store was **repositioning** itself as a casual clothing company, not simply collegiate apparel and funny t-shirts company, this was a change we all supported. It seemed like the right time. The new logo had more modern block lettering, was easier to read, and gave our store more of an upscale look. This was the beginning of what seemed to be the company trading up to a new set of customers.

The roll out also included a new website, which was used to counter the company's lack of a strong **advertising budget**. Local radio ads were often placed for store openings or big events, but most of our pro-motion was done through word-of-mouth and exposure on TV shows. The problem with our new website was that, unlike the growing pop-ularity of major online retailers, our website didn't have any capability of ordering any of our products. The site showcased our products with the intention of driving customers to stores instead of selling directly to consumers. This concerned us in the stores because we knew that our store needed to be constantly visually appealing and well stocked, which is no small feat for a store manager.

When I was first transferred to this store, I can remember thinking that there was absolutely no way that I would be able to make a dent in the amount of work that it would take to get this store up and run-ning. The stockroom had no visible system of organization, as boxes just seemed to be placed randomly throughout this gigantic backroom. The Starbury shoes, which were in the far back corner of the store near the stockroom entrance, were a complete mess. Shoeboxes were scat-tered, shoes were thrown around the floor out of boxes, and it was hard to tell if any shoe in the section had a matching set. I was told that they sold so fast in that store that they just brought them out from the stock room, set them down, and customers bought them right out of the employees' hands.

The rest of the store was also in complete disarray. It was not the fault of the store employees, as many of them were extremely hard working. The only thing that the employees seemed to want from me was a little guidance. The chaos of that store gave every manager who had ever worked there a quick reason to leave the company, and the revolving door of managers made employees feel like they were being thrown to the wolves. One manager arrived in the store from his 2 weeks of New York training, took one look at the store and quit. These hourly employees were capable, just poorly trained and had never had any stable management.

The worst part of the store was the room filled with men's denim. The way our stores were supposed to be merchandised were that denim was placed in one of two ways. Some of the men's jeans were hung on clipped hangers, but the most efficient way to merchandise was to have them neatly folded on tables so that sizes were visible to customers and shopping was made easy. When I first arrived at that store, I saw a wooden pallet sitting on the floor and piles of jeans were thrown on top. None of them were stacked, there was no sizing order or organization of styles. The t-shirt rooms were no better.

One of my first orders of business was to have a quick huddle with my employees and spend some time teaching them the proper way to fold various types of clothing. Short-sleeved and long-sleeved t-shirts both had different methods of being folded so they would fit inside of their cubes. There was a method of folding denim so that it would be neatly arranged on a table, and any item that was on a hanger was placed so that the hanger made a question mark shape. This was to ensure that all hangars faced the right direction. I taught them about how these methods were to make our store look nicer, to make it easier for customers to shop, and to make it easier for employees to keep our store full of the right merchandise. It was incredible how quickly they learned and how a few days later our store was taking shape.

The stockroom was another story altogether, as there was no way this would be a quick or easy fix. I realized quickly that many of the boxes in the stockroom were placed in no visible order, and after opening some of them, I realized that many of the boxes contained various types of merchandise. The system that the company kept track of merchandise by the box. If each box had different types of clothing inside of it, it meant that the entire store was void of any proper inventory count.

Once a year we did a full physical inventory count, counting every item in the entire store. We hired retail merchandising company who had employees trained in inventory counting. Since the previous year's **inventory cycle** took place before this store was opened, no complete physical inventory had ever been performed in this store. I was acutely aware that at no time had this store ever actually had an accurate count of the merchandise on hand.

The only way to fix the inventory problem was to do it in a very meticulous way. We had to open every box, verify its contents, relabel each box, and begin to organize it in a way where all of us knew where we could find the items we needed. I told my employees that once we had a system in place, we could simply keep it going with every truck we received and that we would never be in this situation again. They were excited for the prospect of having some order in the stockroom.

After what seemed like an eternity, we had the store in relative working order. This store was never going to be perfect, but it had come a long way. I was given permission from the company to have an almost limitless amount of **labor hours** in which to get the store up to shape before the Christmas season. My first instinct was to immediately jump at the idea of having a store full of productive employees working at once. At one point we had over 100 hourly employees on our roster.

Recently, the company had moved away from making the manager's bonuses based on scores from visual audits. This couldn't have made me happier, since I can't imagine this store ever successfully passing a visual audit. The new method was going to be more like many other retail stores, and that would be a bonus structure based on labor hours. The company would give us a number of labor hours we had available to schedule, and then we would monitor daily sales and adjust accordingly. **Labor efficiency** was the key. We had to make sure that the amount of employee labor hours we used were under the mark for the daily and weekly sales. If we were successful in keeping our labor in check, managers would receive a bonus to their paychecks.

In my case, I quickly realized how this new bonus structure was probably good for most stores, but would deliver a hard blow to my paychecks. I was given permission from the company to schedule extra employees on each shift so that we could effectively get the store the way that it needed to be. However, my bonus structure still operated as it had before. This means that I would always be over the required **labor ratio**, and I never once received a bonus the entire time I worked at that store. I quickly realized this might have been one of the reasons so many of the managers who worked before me had quit the company soon after starting.

By October, the store seemed to be getting closer to being ready for the holiday season. The additional labor certainly cut into my paycheck, but I was happy seeing that our efforts were starting to pay off. At least from a customer's perspective, our store seemed to be in good working order. We frequently had guests tell us how much easier it was for them to shop in the store, and how they loved how clean and organized it looked. Had they stepped foot in the stockroom they might not have felt that way, but we did our best to keep up with appearances.

One morning, I was radioed by a cashier that I needed to come to the front of the store and approve an **employee discount**. One of the perks to working for our company was that hourly employees got 30% off all their purchases, whereas managers and corporate office employees received 40% off. Considering our already low price points, these discounts made it really attractive for all of us to shop there. Every pair of jeans and khaki pants, every polo shirt, every sweatshirt, every hoodie, and every pair of shoes I owned at one point was purchased from the store I worked in. I often felt like a walking billboard for Steve and Barry's.

Our process for ringing up merchandise with a discount was simple. A manager would come to the cash register and approve any purchases made with a discount. I would have to type in my employee password to activate the discount, log it into a book, and save a copy of the receipt. If the employee worked for corporate or another store, all we had to do was make a phone call to verify. At the end of the night, we would compare our log with a computer print-out of discounts given. If the two matched, we knew every discount was accounted for.

When I reached the cash registers, I saw a middle-aged woman I didn't recognize. I greeted her and she told me that she worked for the corporate office and she just wanted to get her discount as she was doing some shopping for her family. She proceeded to tell me that she grew up near there, and her family still lived nearby. She had worked on Long Island for many years, and had worked for Steve and Barry's for the last two.

"So, is your store pretty excited yet?" she asked me.

"About the holidays? Sure! We've worked so hard to get our store in order and we are all sure we will have a great holiday season" I quickly replied.

"No, are you excited about Amanda Bynes?" she clarified. I assumed she meant her new line of clothing. "Amanda Bynes is doing a store signing in your store next week. Surely, being the store manager, you know about that."

I can't imagine the dumbfounded look on my face. "I don't know what you're talking about, but you obviously have the wrong store. There's absolutely no way Amanda Bynes is coming to this store. First, the entire company knows that this store was in disarray, the staff is young and overworked, and there's no way we wouldn't be given time to prepare." I told her.

"I told you, I work in the corporate office. I know exactly where Amanda Bynes is going to be next week. She's going on a full tour to promote her 'Dear' line, and this store is one of her first stops. Maybe you should make a few phone calls and get up to speed." As I signed off on her discount, I still thought she was the one who was misinformed.

I made the trek across my large store to the manager's office and picked up the phone and called Beverly, my district manager, and told her about the conversation I had. Beverly got a good laugh about it and told me to not even think twice about that conversation, as there's absolutely no way Amanda Bynes was coming to our store. I told her that this woman seemed quite convinced, and maybe she should make a few phone calls to double check. Beverly called her boss, and was told the same thing. Amanda Bynes was certainly not coming to my store next week.

I breathed a sigh of relief. This was the first time I was glad that when it seemed like a member of the corporate office didn't know what was going on in stores. After my experience with a store signing for Stephon Marbury, having Amanda Bynes in the store was not something any of us wanted. Though it sounded exciting, my employees and I all agreed that exciting was the last thing our store needed.

Chapter 12 Key Terms

1. Advertising
2. Employee discount
3. Inventory cycle
4. Labor efficiency
5. Labor hours
6. Labor ratio

7. Position (Positioning)
8. Reposition
9. Revenue

Chapter Takeaways

- Even successful companies can use a facelift. Steve and Barry's worked to attract new customers by repositioning their company. A new logo and company name were among the efforts.
- A website was launched, but it lacked the ability to see any products to customers.
- Manager's bonuses were now determined by their use of labor. However, it was not possible for some managers to ever receive a bonus based on this system.

Discussion Questions

1. How did Steve and Barry's attempt to reposition the company? Do you agree with this move? Why or why not?
2. Explain how the managers' bonuses were now structured. Do you think this was fair? Why or why not?
3. The author mentions the amount of work it took to get the store in order. What were some of the tasks required to do this?
4. Why did the author not believe the employee who informed him of the celebrity event? Would you have believed them? Why or why not?

Employee Relations

I hung up the phone with Beverly and grabbed my lunch out of the refrigerator. As much as I felt a hot lunch out was well deserved, I was the only manager on duty at the time. I couldn't leave the store. Our policy was there always needed to be a manager in the store. If there weren't any other managers or keyholders working at the time, it meant I'd have to take my lunch in the office. This often felt like more of a working lunch than an actual break, as I'd try to eat a sandwich while counting down a cash register or moving boxes in the backroom. Nothing made employees need my attention more than taking a bite. That day I got to sit alone, eat a peanut butter and jelly sandwich and have a few minutes of solitude. Then I was told over the walkie-talkie that Beverly was on the phone and needed to talk to me.

"The **regional manager** just got off the phone with corporate and that woman who was in your store was right. Amanda Bynes is coming to your store next week for a signing and I have no idea who messed up but they forgot to tell me. I'm not sure what we are going to do but I'll be calling back shortly."

I hung up the phone and just stared at the receiver for the next few minutes. I ran out to the front of the store and looked at the first employee that I could find and told her the news. I then called the rest of the store to come to a huddle so I could tell them all as soon as possible. I didn't want my employees going one more day without knowing what was about to happen.

The hours I had been working recently were draining every bit of energy I had left in me. I tried every day to come to work and try to inspire the store to give it their best shot, but I found I was running out of pep talks. I had been working 15–18 hours a day, at minimum 6 days a week, sometimes 7. I had received a small percentage raise to my **base salary** that year, but without the opportunity to receive any bonuses, I realized I was making less money than I had the year before. I was working a lot harder and for far more hours.

If I did get a day off at this point, I would come home and keep my cell phone turned off or on silent. I didn't have a corporate cell phone, nor did I have any type of home landline. I knew if I left the phone on someone from work would either call me to ask me questions or try to get me to come in on my days off. I learned it was best to simply keep it off. Beverly told me she needed me to be available on my days off, but I knew I needed an adjustment to my **work-life balance**. I remained unreachable on my days off.

The previous year I had started looking into applying to law school. I was interested in continuing my education beyond my MBA, and thought the possibility of attending law school might make sense. I was a good student, and knew that I'd likely do very well if I was accepted. I didn't think the world needed another lawyer, but I knew I needed a change.

When I explained to Beverly that I wanted to enroll in law school, I was sure to explain I would be doing so part-time. I told her how it was an evening program and would only require me to be in class 2 nights a week and that I could easily work around that. I told her I'd find my own time to study, and that I didn't expect any sort of **tuition reimbursement** from them. I explained that I thought that maybe I could be a great asset to the company after I graduated. I had worked full-time in graduate school. I could do it again.

Without hesitation she explained under no circumstances would the company allow any of their salaried employees to have anything but a completely open schedule. If I wanted to enroll in night school, I'd have to leave the company. In 2006, I made the decision to put law school on hold and stay with the company. By October of 2007, I was regretting this decision every single day. Turning my phone off seemed to make me feel like it was one way I was controlling my own life.

When Beverly explained to me the plan to prepare for the in-store signing, I knew my body wasn't going to agree with whatever she was about to say. I was mentally and physically exhausted. I had never experienced **work burnout** to this level before. I had always found a way to push through long hours, but I think it was a combination of going for so long and frustration with the company itself.

Beverly explained that she would be driving out to our store and that she would stay in a local hotel and work out of our store every day until event took place. We would also be host to one of the lead **visual merchandising designers**. He would be flying out and working with us. She explained that he played an integral role in the clothing lines and how they were displayed in our stores. She said he was the best person in the entire company to help get our store looking perfect.

She told me that I'd have to work more hours than I had been, and that I would have to schedule my part time employees more than I ever had, but that her reputation was on the line so we had to make it work. I wasn't sure what she meant by working more hours than I had, I assumed she simply didn't realize how much time I had been working. I felt I had been given an unmanageable **workload** and was about to break.

The next day, Beverly arrived at the store with Ben, the visual merchandising designer. They both walked in with breakfast for themselves from a local fast food restaurant. I walked them to the back office and the first thing Ben did was throw his breakfast in the trash. He hadn't even opened the bag, but told me that he had changed his mind and that he would order breakfast from somewhere else. It was clear that the company was paying for it, and he was not interested in saving the company money. It was hard for me to not try to eat the food myself.

Beverly seemed visibly on edge, and seemed especially unhappy with me. She proceeded to tell me that when I left today, that she would expect me back at 5 p.m. I told her that if I'm working through the night, that I usually come in at 10:00 p.m. and stay through the morning. I would come to realize my new schedule was to come in at 5 p.m., work through the night and stay until noon the next day. I found out this was meant to be 7 days a week, and that I just simply was going to have to learn to cope with working 19-hour days. Beverly also had no intention of this schedule stopping after the autograph signing, but that it would continue through the new year.

"Look Beverly, I've always done whatever it takes to make sure things worked out. When you transferred me here, I started working a lot more hours than I ever did before. I never got a raise for coming here, and I'm not paid a penny extra to work these extra hours. Since coming here, I've lost any opportunity to even get any bonus pay. I think working that much is a little unreasonable." I did my best to plead my case to her.

"This is your job and it appears you need to get your priorities in order. That's your schedule, and I expect you to work it." She told me. I left that conversation trying to figure out what my actual priorities really were. I was beginning to believe that this store wasn't any longer one of mine. Maybe my own physical and mental health should be my priority instead. I knew I needed a more positive **work environment**.

I worked the best that my body would allow. Ben had demanded a lot of changes he wanted us to make to our store, and repeatedly told me how ashamed he was of us allowing his company to look like our store did. He was never shy about telling me how terrible our store was. I often tried to explain the store that I inherited and how much progress we had made, but Ben never wanted to hear them. He simply told me that the company should be ashamed.

The last time I saw him was on a Friday, the day before the big autograph signing was to take place. It was around 11:00 a.m., and I had been in the store since 5 p.m. the night before. I was tired, upset, and knew I needed a shower as much as a cup of coffee. On any other day, my tolerance level for small things might have been higher, but not on this day. I was beyond my breaking point.

Ben walked up to a rack of women's shirts and looked at it in disgust. He pushed the entire rack of clothing over onto the floor, snapped his fingers at the nearest hourly employee he could find. In this case, it was a 16-year-old female that had just been hired that week. She was working hard, but was intimidated by the fast pace of the store. He said to her "You, pick this rack of clothes up, and hang the shirts on it right. If you do it wrong, I'll make you do it again."

I was only a few feet away, and was immediately furious. I had always tried to maintain positive **employee relations** and wasn't about to let this happen. I walked directly over to my employee and quietly told her that she could go back to what she was doing and not to worry about those shirts. I assured her it was OK and she could go back to what she was doing. I again told her not to worry about it.

"Look, I don't care who you think you are, but this is my store, not yours. You might refer to this as your company, but this is my store. You will not snap your fingers at my employees. You will not talk down to my employees, in fact you will not talk to my employees at all. If you want any of my employees to do anything, you will come to me and I will let them know what they need to do. If you have a problem, you will take it up with me and no one else." I stormed off to the back of the store, went in the manager's office and started thinking about what my priorities just might be.

I kept to myself for another hour, enough to allow myself to calm down. I clocked out around noon, and left for my drive home. I had an hour commute each way, as the traffic was always heavy in that area. On my drive home, stuck in traffic, I came to the realization that my priorities would never again include Steve and Barry's. I had reached my breaking point, and I knew that it was over. As soon as I got home, I tore a piece of paper out of a notebook, grabbed a pen, and scribbled down the first thing that came to mind.

After a shower, a meal, and a nap, I drove back to the store. I walked in and went straight to the manager's office. I saw Beverly standing there talking to another manager. I didn't look at either of them, nor did I say a word. I thought I heard one of them talking to me, but I couldn't make out anything they said. It was probably just them saying hello, but I never actually heard what it was they said. I gently set my keys on the table, and propped the note up right next to it. I turned, walked out of the office and continued out the front door.

Chapter 13 Key Terms

1. Base salary
2. Employee relations
3. Regional manager
4. Tuition reimbursement
5. Visual merchandising designer
6. Work burnout
7. Work environment
8. Work-life balance
9. Workload

Chapter Takeaways

- Employee burnout can be serious and can cause any employee to lose trust in their organization.
- A successful organization should respect a positive work-life balance for their employees.
- Employee relations, at all levels within the organization, must be a priority for any organization.

Discussion Questions

1. The author, as well as his district manager, did not have sufficient notice about the upcoming event. What steps did the company try to take to prepare?
2. The author writes about his burnout. What factors led to him reaching that point?

3. How do you feel about Ben, the visual merchandising director? How would you have handled working with him?
4. What were the employee relations like within the company? How could they have been more positive?

I Quit

I wrote the words on a piece of paper with a bold black sharpie. "Dear Beverly, you told me to get my priorities straight. That's exactly what I've done. Sometimes the only way up is out. I quit."

Leaving Steve and Barry's wasn't an easy decision. I had always given employers a **two-week notice**. I had just resigned the night before a big event. Leaving the company had been on my mind for some time, but I couldn't help but feel like I had made the decision too quickly. I worried if my decision was made in haste, or if it was fueled by anger or exhaustion. I felt both joy and guilt that I should have been working tirelessly through the night to prepare the store for what was surely going to be a huge event. Instead, I was sitting in my apartment watching old reruns on TV.

The next morning, I decided to drive by the store just to see if there was any commotion, but quickly talked myself out of getting out of bed. I hadn't gotten a full night's sleep in so long that my own legs were telling me not to get up. I turned on the local network news affiliate channel to see if any reporters were covering the store event. I watched for an hour or two, and never saw the store mentioned. The next morning,

I picked up the Sunday paper and never saw one mention of Steve and Barry's or Amanda Bynes.

I never found out if the store was prepared for her to show up, nor did I ever know if there was even someone at the store ready to open the doors for her. I never found out if the event took place. I never followed up with anyone in that store, nor have I spoken to anyone in that store since I walked out. My resignation wasn't on good terms.

Before I left the company, there was discussion of the company becoming publicly traded. When I had visited the corporate office, I had been told that executives were meeting with potential investors to discuss the possibility. After that, many of the communications we received at store level mentioned all our hard work would pay off when the company went public. There were so many rumors circulating. It served as an incentive for us to work harder, longer, and to want to be a part of that company for as long as possible.

My last 6 months in the store made me believe that there was no way our company would ever become publicly traded, and my feelings were proven to be right. Despite the company's efforts, they were never able to make it to the New York Stock Exchange. By the end of 2008, Steve and Barry's had closed their stores nationwide and went out of business. When I first heard about the store closing, I felt like I was right about walking out the front door.

Then I felt a rush of sadness overcome me. I stopped what I was doing, and almost broke down and cried. Steve and Barry's had given so many people a great place to shop. It allowed so many pairs of shoes to make it into the hands of people who before would have never been able to afford them. They had shown the entire retail world that you can sell great clothing for a reasonable price. It gave us all a place to find a t-shirt that we could wear to the bar and get a few laughs from anyone who saw it. It was truly a remarkable store for anyone who had the chance to shop in one.

I spent the next few months working for another retail company, but 2008 would prove to be the last time I worked in retail in any sort of managerial capacity. Since leaving Steve and Barry's, I still find myself overwhelmed with memories of working there. Some were good, some were even fun, and others tire me out just to think about them. Steve and Barry's was a company that was started by two amazing entrepreneurs who wanted to change retail forever. It was a good company that could have been great, and should have become one of the most successful companies in history.

Instead, Steve and Barry's became nothing more than a distant memory for me. My time with Steve and Barry's was short, though 2 years seemed like an eternity. I never knew everything that happened behind every closed door, or how the decisions were made at the corporate level. I will never know what the real reasons were why the company was never able to go public. I don't feel I can take credit for any of the amazing success, or failure, of the company. To this day, I feel like someone who was simply along for the ride.

I did, however, have a great chance to experience the company in a way that not many people could. I spent time at the corporate office, and even went through interviews for an executive position. I watched our stores struggle with information, and experienced first-hand the times we felt helpless to make our stores work. I got to see the good and bad decisions put to the test, and have spent over a decade replaying them in my head and truly trying to make sense of it all.

I owe a lot to Steve and Barry's. They hired me shortly after finishing graduate school and allowed me to put a roof over my head for two years. They gave me my first salaried job, and provided me for the first time with health insurance and benefits. They gave me the opportunity to manage multiple stores, and work with hundreds of employees. I also learned a lot about how to grow, how to nurture, and how to sink a company. Sometimes the best lessons we learn in life are some of the hardest ones. We can always learn more from failure than from success.

Over a decade after the last Steve and Barry's store has closed, there have been drastic changes in the society. I still always go out on Black Friday, but instead of a large crowd and doorbuster sales, most of us stay home and shop from our phones. Instead of renting movies from a local video store, most of us simply choose to stream them. Social media is where we get our news, where we make our friends, and where we tell each other about ourselves. We are rated by our number of followers, views, and likes.

It's hard to say where the next big revolution in retail will happen, or whether it will happen slowly or abruptly. Personally, I hope another store like Steve and Barry's comes around. I would love to see some entrepreneurs not only attempt to change the game, but to succeed. I hope to see companies challenge the status quo, be different, and be themselves. It won't be me working in the stores, but I hope their managers are ready to take a ride.

Glossary of Terms

3rd quarter the months of July, August, and September.

4th quarter the months of October, November, and December. In most retail stores it is the busiest part of the year.

Advertising a set amount of money allocated by a company to use for advertising.

Alarm services company a company who provides an electronic alarm system.

Assigning shifts a step in employee scheduling when individual employees are assigned to work specific times.

Base salary the amount of money earned before any bonus was applied.

Benefits additional compensation in addition to salary or wage. Often includes health insurance, paid time off, or other forms of compensation.

Big-box retailer large retailers.

Black Friday the nickname for the day after Thanksgiving that marks the beginning of the retail shopping holidays.

Board room a room in which the board, or higher-level executives within a company meet.

Bonus structure a form of compensation designed to reward performance.

Business hours the times when the store is open for business.

Calling-off calling your employer to report that you will not be coming to work for your shift.

Cash handling procedures a set of procedures designed to improve the efficiency and reduce error in cash handling.

Ceiling-hung signs large signs that are suspended from the ceiling that can be seen across the store.

Celebrity endorsement a financial partnership with a famous person directly tied to a specific product or brand.

Closing shift a shift that works until the store closes for the day.

Code word a word or phrase spoken by employees to alert management or other employees without a customer knowing its meaning.

Commercial shipping company a company whose primary business is shipping merchandise for other companies. Also referred to as trucking company.

Company executive the highest-level employees who oversee the overall company.

Company newsletter a periodically released bulletin for members within an organization.

Conference call a business meeting held remotely over the phone that often includes upper management and store-level employees.

Corporate communications messages released by a company both within the company and externally to the public.

Costume jewelry inexpensive jewelry with little value.

Counting up (drawer) procedures required to prepare a cash drawer for an employee to use. Usually includes counting the physical currency and other store specific procedures.

Demographics a group of consumers characterized by factors such as age, ethnicity, gender, level of education, and income level.

Department a specific part of the store that housed one grouping of items.

Direct deposit an agreement with a company that allows your paychecks to be automatically deposited into your bank account.

District manager a manager whose job is to oversee multiple stores in each district.

Divider a marked barrier that divides inventory for different stores within the same truck.

Door buster a type of sale that is for a limited time and starts when the store opens.

Employee discount a company provided benefit to employees where they can receive a discount on in-store merchandise.

Employee incentive a reward for employees to perform certain tasks.

Employee morale the attitude or happiness of employees.

Employee relations a focus on positive relationships between the company and its employees.

Employee screening processes used to determine if an applicant has the qualifications to work for an organization.

Employee turnover the rate at which employees leave an organization, whether voluntarily or involuntarily, and are replaced by new employees.

End caps a type of shelving unit display placed at the end of shelving units or aisles.

External candidates applicants, or potential applicants, for a position that do not work for the organization.

External theft theft committed by people outside of the company.

Free-standing display units types of displays that stand on their own unattached to other displays or shelves.

Handler a personal assistant to a celebrity or important person.

Head cashier a cashier promotion that allows for more store leadership within their current position.

Holiday bonus a practice among some employers where an employee is paid an additional lump sum of money during the holiday season.

Hourly employee an employee paid based on the amount of time they worked. Generally broken up into hours.

Individual alarm code in most retail companies, managers are each given a unique code to arm and disarm the security system.

Internal theft theft committed by employees or people within the organization.

Intranet a computer network designed to be used for communications within the company.

Inventory control system a system designed to keep track of merchandise in the store.

Inventory cycle average inventory levels compared to average sales.

Itemized log a list of all merchandise received listed individually.

Job description a written set of details regarding the specific requirements and scope of a position within a company.

Job promotion an employee obtains a new job, title, or status within a company that would increase their position in the organizational hierarchy.

Job reference a person who has the ability to speak, or write, on your behalf in regards to your experience or character. Usually used during a job application.

Just-in-time performing tasks as they are needed.

Keyholder a store leader who is given managerial authority within the store without being a full-time manager.

Labor efficiency the amount of labor hours used compared to the number of daily sales.

Labor hours the amount of time worked by the employees in a given period.

Labor ratio the amount a money a company spends on employees compared to the sales.

Licensed apparel clothing that contains a brand that the manufacturer was given legal permission to use.

Loss prevention also known as asset protection. Steps made by a company to prevent or reduce profit or revenue loss.

Loss prevention employee an employee whose job is to prevent losses, usually by monitoring the store for theft.

Manager-on-duty the manager currently in charge of the store at a given time.

Market share the percentage of the total market controlled by one company.

MBA a master's degree in business administration.

Media Exposure attention and coverage from media sources such as radio and television.

Minimum wage the lowest hourly wage allowed by law.

nine-to-five job a job that an employee works a regular schedule. Usually refers to Monday through Friday from 9 a.m. until 5 p.m.

No-call no-show an employee failing to report to work for their shift without notifying the company.

Paid time off a benefit to some employees that allows them to get paid for a certain number of days that they don't have to report to work. Can include pay for sick leave or vacation.

Panic button a button, usually in a hidden spot beneath the cash register that an employee can press to silently alert the authorities during a robbery.

Personal days a type of paid time off that an employee can use for time off when they aren't sick.

Physical count the process of counting every item received or on the shelf.

Physical security system a common tool for loss prevention that includes anti-theft devices and cameras.

Pilfering stealing small items.

Point of sale (POS) the point of the store that customers purchase items. Usually includes a cash register.

Point-of-purchase signage any type of merchandising located on or near the cash registers.

Position (Positioning) value observed by a target market.

Price ceiling the highest price charged for an item or group of items.

Price point the standard price for items sold.

Price strategy using the price of items in a strategic manner to generate sales.

Price war a phenomenon when multiple businesses attempt to undercut each other's prices often resulting in artificially low prices.

Product line a group of products that are sold under one brand name.

Products merchandise within a store.

Profitability the level in which a company earns a profit.

Promoting from within providing promotion opportunities for current employees.

Punctuality arriving (to work) on-time.

Pushing a market a strategy for a company to attempt to get their message to potential consumers.

Quid pro quo granting a favor with the expectation of a returned favor.

Receiving (location) the location within the store, usually in the stockroom, that merchandise enters the store.

Receiving inventory a system of physical acquiring and counting merchandise that arrives in the store.

Recruiter someone whose job is to locate potential employees.

Regional manager A manager who oversees a large region of stores. Generally, the direct supervisor to the district manager.

Reposition attempts to change the position of the company to its target market or change the target market.

Retail a business whose primary customer is the final user of a product.

Retail lease a contractual agreement to pay a landlord for the use of retail space.

Retail management the management of retail companies.

Retail security actions and procedures designed to keep employees and merchandise safe.

Revenue sales generated by a company.

Salary a form of employee compensation in which an employee is paid a flat rate regardless of hours worked.

Security alarm a type of alarm that is used when the store is closed and empty. Typically notifies the authorities if it is set off.

Shoplifter/shoplifting a person who steals from a store.

Shopping center a grouping of separated retail outlets.

Shrinkage loss by a company often a result of shoplifting.

Sick days a type of paid time off that is used exclusively for when an employee is sick.

Stage prepare something to be used at a later date.

Start-of-shift huddle a gathering of employees, usually in a circle, where a manager explains daily tasks and attempts to inspire the team.

stock keeping unit (SKU) a bar code or an item number used to identify a specific size, color, or type of product within a store.

Stockroom employee employee whose job is to organize and fill the stockroom.

Store layout the design of the physical areas within the store.

Store management retail managers who work in a store and whose primary duties are to manage the store they are assigned.

Store opening procedures the series of tasks required to open a store for the day's business.

Store opening team employees whose job is to set up and prepare a new store to open for business.

Store-level employees any employees, whether hourly or management, that work within a given store.

Take-home-pay a slang term for a paycheck after taxes and other deductions.

Target market the group of consumers that a company chooses to be the focus of a product.

Targeting focusing on a specific segment of customers.

Time and a half when an employee is paid 150% of their usual hourly wage.

Time theft stealing company time by being on the clock when an employee isn't working.

Training director an employee whose job is to oversee and develop training programs within a company.

Trend (trendy) something that is popular.

Truck receiving the process of unloading physical merchandise from a distribution truck.

Tuition reimbursement an employer repays all or some of an employee's tuition expenses.

Visual audit a type of audit designed to check the visual appearance of a store.

Visual merchandising designer an employee whose job is to create visual displays and other visual elements to a store.

Work burnout the point at which an employee reaches the point of mental and/or physical exhaustion from their job.

Work environment the physical, mental and social conditions of a workplace.

Work-life balance the balance between time spent working and time spent away from work.

Workload the amount of work or responsibilities that are placed upon an individual employee.